Nothing Like
it Before

Library of Congress Catalog Card Number 98-66341

ISBN: 978-2765-01-5

Book Layout and Typesetting by Designer Supplements, Woodbridge, Virginia   USA

Distribution and Orders

Published and Distributed by Royal Productions. Please address all inquiries and orders to:

Royal Productions *(Publishers)*
7127 Little River Turnpike, Suite 205
Annandale, Virginia 22003
USA

Tel: 703 750-1596

Fax: 703 916-7773

E-Mail: twmgroup@ipo.net

Contents

Foreword

Soccer is everywhere. Its range encompasses the South American Amazon rainforests to the remote interiors of Africa. Peoples from the dry climate of the Arabian desert to the temperate zones of Europe, the tundras of Scandinavia, and the rainy cobblestones of the United Kingdom celebrate this popular sport. One can cross the Himalayas into China, Japan, all of Southeast Asia, then sail to Australia and New Zealand and find filled sports arenas where soccer is played. Even countries of the Western hemisphere, north and south, have embraced the old "football": Canada, the United States, Mexico, and the Caribbean. SOCCER IS NOW THE INTERNATIONAL SUPREME SPORT.

Today, soccer has also taken root in our communities of women. The prestige of the sport has grown beyond the boundaries of male-only competition, helping to create a sense of purpose by allowing athletes to contribute to civilization as equals. Soccer is still the leading international barrier breaker which has attracted millions as players, and as spectators cheering for their beloved teams.

With mass media "satellites" beaming communications throughout the world, soccer has surpassed most other major sports in popularity. It is played seven days a week, and promoted on all six continents for its millions of fans. As a result of the worldwide interest in this billion-dollar profit sporting event, many associations sponsor the development of soccer, from basic to professional levels.

Besides the physical and mental conditioning required for the players, referees, and organizers of soccer tournaments, there is an intercultural aspect which draws a great deal of attention to the character formation of its players and associated bodies. Therefore, we can address soccer as we do other victorious major sporting events: soccer is an INTERNATIONAL LANGUAGE.

This book is written to present a broader scope of what soccer means to all persons who want to learn about this popular sport. It is a story that gives the reader a front row view of all the exciting moments of soccer.

Mal Whitfield, 1948 & 1952 Olympic Gold Medalist
The Whitfield Foundation, Washington, D.C.

ACKNOWLEDGEMENTS

I gratefully acknowledge the assistance I received from various persons in several countries I visited in the course of researching and verifying facts and figures about ancient soccer and the World Cup Championships. In this regard, particular mention must be made of Mr. Joseph S. Blatter, formerly Secretary-General and now president of the Federation of International Football Associations (FIFA) for answering some seemingly intractable questions I had on the global tournament. The brief interview I had with him after a news conference at the Hotel Le Meridien in Paris, France on March 10, 1998 was very insightful.

Mr. Jacques Lambert, Managing Director of the French Organising Committee (CFO) of the 1998 World Cup, also deserves a special commendation for facilitating my uphill research task. Responding in English sometimes and French at other times, Mr. Lambert answered all the nagging questions I had about the CFO, the sponsors and marketing partners. The CFO Press Officer, Mr. Laurent Chetrit, must be recognized for his price-less assistance in accessing useful material on the World Cup.

What shall I say about the Yugoslav Coach Slobodan Santraç alias Sani and the General Secretary of Yugoslavia Football Association Branko Bulatovic? Words are not enough to express adequate appreciation to them for the extra mile they went to provide information and validate needed facts and figures during an interview that lasted from midnight to 4:00 a.m.

Carlos Alberto Parreira, the ebullient coach who won the 1994 World Cup championship for Brazil, must be thanked for granting me a brief interview in Paris, soon after taking over as trainer of the Saudi Arabian World Cup squad.

I am indebted to Reverend Colin & Isabel Davey, Alan Sobey and members of the Queens Street Baptist Church in Erith, England for receiving me with their hearts and especially for allowing me to use their computer only one day after I met them, while on a research trip to London.

The chairman of the Nigerian Football Association (NFA), retired Colonel A. M. Aminu, the Secretary General Sani Toro and police chief M. D. Abubakar deserve pats on the back for their assistance.

I acknowledge the various contributions Barbara Carpenter and Mrs. Susan Grady made towards the production of this research effort.

My profound thanks also go to some diplomats and embassy officials in Washington, D.C., who spared time to confirm some facts and figures on soccer relating to their various countries. In this wise, special mention must be made of Mr. Liu Zhengrong of the Chinese Embassy, Miss Makiko Uemura of Japan, and Mechtild Ewert of the German Embassy. The fact checking assistance I received from Connie Mourtoupalas at the Embassy of Greece, Eduardo Rosenbrock at the Embassy of Uruguay, and Anne Volpert and Patrick Juillard of the French Embassy was invaluable.

I must pay tribute to Mr. Sam H. Ka of the Korean Football Association, Jo Gibbons, Press Officer with England's 2006 World Cup Campaign Team, Mr. Clay Burton of U.S. Parcel in Springfield, Virginia, and members of my family for their assistance with fact checking and preparation of the manuscript.

Above all, to God be the glory and praise for making possible the successful execution of a project that seemed unattainable at the onset.

Washington, D.C.   May 1998

Dedication

Dedicated to all lovers of sports around the world
and to the players, coaches, and fans, as well as
their parents, sons and daughters.

In a grand style reminiscent of the amazing soccer artistry of his heyday, the wondrous right foot of World Cup soccer legend, Pele (right), gets entangled with the left foot of U.S. President Bill Clinton (left) in Rio de Janeiro during a one-on-one round of soccer to the delight of a multitude of school kids and dignitaries.

The event was recorded during the visit of President Clinton to Brazil on October 15, 1997. President Clinton had visited the "Vila Olimpica", a sports-oriented school, located in a Rio suburb.
Accompanied by Pele on the visit, President Clinton played a brief round of one-on-one soccer with the Brazilian idol and netted a point-blank goal against a budding young star of the school for the poor in another round with the students.

Afterwards, President Clinton spoke some words of encouragement to the children saying, "every child enters this world with a gift from God, the power to dream [of great things to achieve] …"

The Untold Stories OF THE World Cup Soccer championships

Fidelis W. Iyebote

Royal Productions

Annandale • Washington DC • London • Paris • Port Harcourt

 **CHAPTER ONE**

THE LAST CHAMPIONSHIP
IN THE 20TH CENTURY

FRANCE 98: THE XVI WORLD CUP

France '98! World Soccer returns to the native land of its originators. June 10 to July 12: The World Soccer Family converges at the home of the founding fathers to celebrate an unsurpassable feast. No other sporting or world event can match its grandeur and popularity. It promises to be a festivity par excellence – one of pomp, fun and tremendous opportunities for peoples of the world to build bridges of understanding, love and friendship across ethnic, racial, religious and cultural lines. The XVI World Cup tournament! Here it comes, helping to bring to the port of realization the hopes of millions from all around the world. It's a dream come true.

Are there good grounds indeed for celebrating? Absolutely yes! Very good reasons, too. From a shaky start in 1904, dogged by an unabatingly hazy future even by May 26, 1928, when a wobbly Federation of International Football Associations (FIFA) resolved to stage a global soccer tournament, FIFA has waxed so strong that its baby – the quadrennial FIFA World Cup championship – is the most glamorous and attractive sporting event under the sun, lustily drawing an estimated 37 billion television viewers in cumulative audience.

At the qualifying stage of the tournament, 172 nations from all over the world contested keenly for the 32 slots to play in the finals. What about the game itself? Soccer is indisputably the king of sports – the most popular, verily artful, a thriller and a great delight to watch. Current data show that it is played in all the nations of the world by 250 million persons, among them 30 million girls and women. Anything like it? Certainly no!

Stade de France, in Saint-Denis, venue of the opening ceremony and the championship game of the XVI World Cup soccer tournament. Construction of the multi-purpose sports arena started in May 1995 and was commissioned in January 1998. The stadium was built at a cost of 2.6 billion French Francs (about 450 million U.S. Dollars). Photo: French Organising Committee (CFO) of the 1998 World Cup

FIFA, soccer and the World Cup Championships have shot from one milestone to another. It has been a phenomenal growth! From a tottering body of seven members – France, Belgium, Denmark, Sweden, the Netherlands, Spain and Switzerland – in 1904, FIFA now has nearly 200 nations as members or affiliates. To whom does the world owe a debt of gratitude for sowing the seeds that have yielded these wonderful fruits? French visionaries – Robert Guerin, a journalist, Henri Delaunay and of course Jules Rimet of blessed memory.

The global soccer association, known everywhere as FIFA, and its brainchild, the World Cup championship are all glaring and glowing testimonies to the love for the game, the love for mankind, statesmanship and hard work this great French trio has shown and left for posterity. The World Cup tourney: Yes! It is a grand exaltation of the pioneering works and selflessness of these illustrious Frenchmen. Without doubt, it is a deserving posthumous accolade. How can anyone fail to recognize it? For, this global soccer festival was a baby born out of their foresight, zeal, sweat and unrelenting efforts.

XVI World Cup Title Contenders
The 32 nations for the FINALS

GROUP A	GROUP B	GROUP C	GROUP D
1 Brazil (BRA) [1]	1 Italy (ITA) [5]	1 France (FRA)	1 Spain (ESP)
2 Scotland (SCO) [2]	2 Chile (CHI) [6]	2 South Africa (RSA)	2 Nigeria (NGA)
3 Morocco (MOR) [3]	3 Cameroon (CMR) [7]	3 Saudi Arabia (KSA)	3 Paraguay (PAR)
4 Norway (NOR) [4]	4 Austria (AUT) [8]	4 Denmark (DEN)	4 Bulgaria (BGR)
GROUP E	**GROUP F**	**GROUP G**	**GROUP H**
1 Netherlands (HOL)	1 Germany (GER)	1 Romania (ROM)	1 Argentina (ARG)
2 Belgium (BEL)	2 United States (USA)	2 Colombia (COL)	2 Japan (JPN)
3 Republic of Korea (KOR)	3 Yugoslavia (YUG)	3 England (ENG)	3 Jamaica (JAM)
4 Mexico (MEX)	4 Iran (IRN)	4 Tunisia (TUN)	4 Croatia (HRV)

France '98 marks the first time as many as 32 countries will be locking horns for this much-coveted trophy – the FIFA World Cup – since the inception of the Championships in Uruguay in 1930. It also goes into the records as the premier occasion that the contestants in the finals are grouped into more than six groups, which was the format in USA '94 and since the XII edition of the World Cup tournament in Spain in 1982.

Europe, with 15 finalists had 50 entries, but 35 of the nations fell by the wayside. Ten South American countries vied for placing in the finals, but only four qualified, making the Latin American slots five, with the inclusion of the reigning champions, Brazil. Africa grabbed five berths, two more than the three slots that the continent was allotted in 1994, although 33 of its 38 entrants were knocked out. Asia started the race with 36 nations, but only four survived to the finals. North and Central America fielded 28 countries, but only three – Mexico, the United States and Jamaica – earned the coveted places. Only Oceania did not produce a finalist, although 10 nations from the Continent participated in the qualifying rounds of the competition!

The draw pitches four nations drawn from the various continents against one another, each team playing three of the total 48 matches in the first round of the tournament. Europe is the only continent with two teams in each group, with the exception of Group H, which has Croatia as the only team from Europe. This is understandable, for Europe entered the largest number of 50 nations for the qualifying rounds and emerged with the highest number of 15 finalists, including the hosts – France.

The FIFA World Cup which replaced the Jules Rimet trophy, won for keeps by Brazil in 1970

1 1

THE TEN VENUES

The 64 matches of the XVI World Cup championship will be played at choice venues in 10 select cities. Nine of the stadia were renovated for the tournament, while the prestigious Stade de France was newly built. The stadia are located in:

Saint-Denis *Stade de France*
Paris *Parc des Princes*
Lens *Stade Félix-Bollaert*
Lyon *Stade de Gerland*
Saint-Etienne *Stade Geoffroy-Guichard*
Marseille *Stade Vélodrome*
Montpellier *Stade de La Mosson*
Toulouse *Stadium Municipal*
Bordeaux *Stade Lescure*
Nantes *Stade de la Beaujoire*

THE DRAW

On December 4, 1997, when the 32 top footballing nations for the XVI World Cup Championships were drawn at Marseille, France into eight groups, the stage was set for the largest and one of the most unpredictable tournaments ever. A record 172 countries began the race for the finals. The qualifying rounds started on March 1, 1996 and ended on November 29, 1997 with the elimination of 140 nations from the series.

Eight nations – Brazil, Italy, France, Spain, The Netherlands, Germany, Romania and Argentina – were seeded. With the exception of Romania, the choice of the top seeds was greeted with considerable approval.

THE ROUND OF SIXTEEN

The sixteen teams – two from each group, that is, the winner of the group and the runners-up – will participate at this stage of the tournament. The Round of Sixteen is scheduled to be played in eight venues – Bordeaux, Lens, Marseille, Montpellier, Paris, Saint-Denis, Saint-Etienne and Toulouse from June 27 to 30.

QUARTER FINALS

Battles in the Quarter Finals will be decided on July 3 and 4 at Marseille, Saint-Denis, Lyon and Nantes.

SEMI-FINALS

The fixtures show that the surviving four teams will lock horns at Marseille and Saint-Denis on July 7 and 8 to determine the two finalists.

THIRD PLACE BATTLE

The battle of the two losing semi finalists for the Third Place is slated for July 11 at the Parc des Princes Stadium in Paris.

THE GRAND FINALE

The winners and runners-up are billed to be decided in the Championships game on July 12 at 21.00 hours European time or 3:00 pm Eastern Standard Time. The venue for the match and the closing ceremonies of the tournament lasting 33 days is the 80,000 capacity Stade de France in Saint-Denis.

First Round Games   XVI FIFA World Cup - France 98   SCHEDULE OF MATCHES

VENUES	Mer Wed 10/06	Jeu Thur 11/06	Ven Fri 12/06	Sam Sat 13/06	Dim Sun 14/06	Lun Mon 15/06	Mar Tues 16/06	Mer Wed 17/06	Jeu Thurs 18/06	Ven Fri 19/06	Sam Sat 20/06	Dim Sun 21/06	Lun Mon 22/06	Mar Tues 23/06	Mer Wed 24/06	Jeu Thurs 25/06	Ven Fri 26/06
Saint-Denis *Stade de France*	Bra/Sco 17H30 01								Fra/Ksa 21H00 21					Ita/Aut 16H00 33			Rom/Tun 21H00 45
Paris *Parc des Princes*						Ger/USA 21H00 14				Nga/Bgr 17H30 23		Arg/Jam 17H30 28				Bel/Kor 16H00 41	
Lens *Stade Félix-Bollaert*			Ksa/Den 17H30 05		Jam/Hrv 21H00 11										Esp/Bgr 21H00 37		Col/Eng 21H00 46
Lyon *Stade de Gerland*				Kor/Mex 17H30 09		Rom/Col 17H30 15						USA/Ira 21H00 30			Fra/Den 16H00 38		Jap/Jam 16H00 47
Saint-Etienne *Stade Geoffroy Guichard*					Yug/Irn 17H30 12			Chi/Aut 17H30 19						Sco/Mor 21H00 34		Hol/Mex 16H00 42	
Marseille *Stade Vélodrome*			Fra/Rsa 21H00 06							Esp/Par 21H00 24	Hol/Kor 21H00 25			Bra/Nor 21H00 35			
Montpellier *Stade de La Mosson*	Mor/Nor 21H00 02			Par/Bgr 14H30 07				Ita/Cmr 21H00 20					Col/Tun 17H30 31			Ger/Irn 21H00 43	
Toulouse *Stadium Municipal*		Cmr/Aut 21H00 03			Arg/Jap 14H30 13				Rsa/Den 17H30 22				Rom/Eng 21H00 32		Nga/Par 21H00 39		
Bordeaux *Stade Lescure*		Ita/Chi 17H30 04					Sco/Nor 14H30 17				Bel/Mex 17H30 26				Rsa/Ksa 16H00 40		Arg/Hrv 16H00 48
Nantes *Stade de la Beaujoire*				Esp/Nga 14H30 10			Bra/Mor 21H00 18				Jap/Hrv 14H30 27			Chi/Cmr 16H00 36		USA/Yug 21H00 44	

14H30 = 8:30am   17H30 = 11:30am   21H00 = 3:00pm

XVI FIFA World Cup - France 98 SCHEDULE OF MATCHES

VENUES	Second Round Fixtures						Quarter Finals				Semi Finals				3d Place	Final
	Sam Sat 27/06	Dim Sun 28/06	Lun Mon 29/06	Mar Tues 30/06	Mer Wed 01/07	Jeu Thurs 02/07	Ven Fri 03/07	Sam Sat 04/07	Dim Sun 05/07	Lun Mon 06/07	Mar Tues 07/07	Mer Wed 08/07	Jeu Thurs 09/07	Ven Fri 10/07	Sam Sat 11/07	Dim Sun 12/07
Saint-Denis *Stade de France*		1D/2C=4 *21H00* 51					2/3=B *16H30* 57					B/D=D2 *21H00* 62				1D1/1D2 *21H00* 64
Paris *Parc des Princes*	1A/2B=1 *21H00* 49														2D1/2D2 *21H00* 63	
Lens *Stade Félix-Bollaert*		1C/2D=3 *16H30* 52														
Lyon *Stade de Gerland*								6/7=D *21H00* 59								
Saint-Etienne *Stade Geoffroy Guichard*				1H/2G=8 *21H00* 55												
Marseille *Stade Vélodrome*	1B/2A=2 *16H30* 50							5/8=C *16H30* 60			A/C=D1 *21H00* 61					
Montpellier *Stade de La Mosson*			1F/2E=6 *16H30* 53													
Toulouse *Stadium Municipal*			1E/2F=5 *21H00* 54													
Bordeaux *Stade Lescure*				1G/2H=7 *16H30* 56			1/4=A *21H00* 58									
Nantes *Stade de la Beaujoire*																

16H30 = 10:30am   21H00 = 3:00pm

 **CHAPTER TWO**

THE WORLD SOCCER FAMILY

A BOND OF FRIENDSHIP AND UNDERSTANDING

The world soccer family comprises approximately 200 member nations who belong to the fold of the Federation of International Football Associations (FIFA). FIFA has nurtured the world soccer family since 1904, begetting members in all Continents of the world. National soccer associations in all the Continents have also constituted themselves into Soccer Confederations. The Confederations organize periodic continental tournaments, bringing together member nations for competitions and "family unions," which foster understanding and strengthen the family relationship.

The Union of European Football Associations (UEFA) is run from Berne, Switzerland. The Confederation of North, Central and Caribbean Football Associations (CONCACAF) has its headquarters in New York, United States and the Asian Football Confederation (AFC) is run from Kuala Lumpur, Malaysia, while the Confederation of African Football Associations (CAF) is administered from Cairo, Egypt, the first African nation to play in the World Cup final stage.

Asunción, Paraguay is home for the Confederation of South American Football Associations (CONMEBOL), while the Oceania Football Confederation (OFC) is administered from Auckland, New Zealand.

FOUNDING FATHERS

The World Soccer family has grown phenomenally from seven members in 1904 to the current 200 nations. More nations are being considered for membership by FIFA. Among the oldest members of the world soccer family are France, Belgium, Denmark, the Netherlands, Spain, Sweden, and Switzerland, whose nationals indeed, founded FIFA.

A UNIFYING FORCE

Sport, particularly soccer, remains one of the world's greatest unifying forces. It is in the arena of sports that most people forget their differences as they converge, talk, make new friends and analyze an impending game or hug, congratulate and commiserate with one another after a won or lost match. Sports indeed bring people together and closer. Soccer builds bridges of contact and understanding among people of different races, ethnicity, tribe, religion, and political persuasion.

Sports help to pull down the strongholds of racism, social, economic, religious and gender discrimination that have bedevilled mankind from time immemorial. An opportunity to come together and exchange ideas before, during and after a game is one that most sports fans would not like to miss for the ignoble reasons of chauvinism and related maladies. Such opportunities herald the beginning of relationships that pave the way for people to know and understand one another. It is a common occurrence to find fans and players jumping at virtually every chance to listen, reason and make friends.

SPORTS DIPLOMACY

The great American track and field star of Olympic fame Mal Whitfield, who is a pundit of sports diplomacy, in an interview, sums it up in these words,"Sports build a society, put people in contact with one another, engender friendship and foster understanding and racial harmony."

Whitfield, a U.S. Gold Medalist in the 1948 London and 1952 Helsinki Olympic Games, believes that politics and ideologies sow seeds of discord among nations and peoples. "What you believe, your political and religious persuasion, may scare away from you people and nations, who don't have the same convictions, if you are not careful," he emphasised.

Almost everybody plays or is a fan of one sport or the other. We all love to play and recreate. Good and famous players of every sport are loved by virtually all in most nations. Fans fraternise with one another and build an array of contacts and relationships in the arena of sports.

Following is a list of FIFA members and affiliates

Europe

France
Belgium
Denmark
The Netherlands
Spain
Sweden
Switzerland
Albania
Andorra
Armenia
Austria
Azores
Bulgaria
Belarus
Bosnia - Herzegovina
Croatia
Cyprus

Czech
England
Estonia
Faroe Islands
Finland
Georgia
Germany
Greece
Hungary
Iceland
Ireland, Northern
Ireland, Republic of
Italy
Latvia
Liechtenstein
Lithuania
Luxembourg

Macedonia (FYR)
Malta
Moldova
Norway
Poland
Portugal
Romania
Russia
San Marino
Scotland
Slovakia
Slovenia
Turkey
Ukraine
Wales
Yugoslavia

North America *(including Central American and Caribbean nations)*

Anguilla
Antigua and Barbuda
Aruba
Bahamas
Barbados
Belize
Bermuda
Canada
Cayman Islands
Costa Rica
Cuba
Dominica

Dominican Republic
El Salvador
Grenada
Guatemala
Guyana
Haiti
Honduras
Jamaica
Mexico
Netherlands Antilles
Nicaragua
Panama

Puerto Rico
St. Kitts and Nevis
St. Lucia
St. Vincent /Grenadines
Suriname
Turks and Caicos
(newest member)
Trinidad and Tobago
United States
Virgin Islands (British)
Virgin Islands (U.S.)

Oceania

American Samoa
Australia
Cook Islands
Fiji
New Caledonia

New Zealand
Niue Island
Northern Marianas
Papua New Guinea
Solomon Islands

Tahiti
Tonga
Vanuatu
Western Samoa

Africa

Algeria	Gabon	Namibia
Angola	Gambia	Niger
Benin	Ghana	Nigeria
Botswana	Guinea	Rwanda
Burkina Faso	Guinea-Bissau	Sao Tome & Principe
Burundi	Ivory Coast	Senegal
Cameroon	Kenya	Seychelles
Cape Verde Islands	Lesotho	Sierra Leone
Central African Republic	Liberia	Somalia
Egypt	Libya	South Africa
Congo DR (formerly Zaire)	Madagascar	Sudan
Republic of Congo	Malawi	Swaziland
Chad	Mali	Tanzania
Djibouti	Mauritania	Togo
Equatorial Guinea	Mauritius	Tunisia
Eritrea	Morocco	Uganda
Ethiopia	Mozambique	Zambia
		Zimbabwe

Asia

Afghanistan	Japan	Oman
Azerbaijan	Jordan	Pakistan
Bahrain	Kazakhstan	Palestine
Bangladesh	Korea DPR (North)	Philippines
Brunei	Korea Republic (South)	Qatar
Cambodia	Kuwait	Saudi Arabia
China PR	Kyrgyzstan	Singapore
Chinese Taipei (Taiwan)	Laos	Sri Lanka
Guam	Lebanon	Syria
Hong Kong	Macao	Thailand
India	Malaysia	Tajikistan
Indonesia	Maldives Republic	Turkmenistan
Iran	Mongolia	United Arab Emirates
Iraq	Myanmar (formerly Burma)	Uzbekistan
Israel	Nepal	Vietnam
		Yemen

South America

Argentina	Colombia	Uruguay
Bolivia	Ecuador	Venezuela
Brazil	Paraguay	
Chile	Peru	

There were 185 member nations of the United Nations as of the autumn of 1997, all of them independent countries. A nation does not have to be independent or self-ruling to be admitted as an affiliate or associate member of the world soccer family. Hence some dependent countries, especially British colonies in Oceania, are associate members of FIFA.

The
32 finalists
and the
**six previous
winners**
of the
World Cup

 1 Brazil (BRA)
 2 Scotland (SCO)
 3 Morocco (MOR)
 4 Norway (NOR)
 5 Italy (ITA)
 6 Chile (CHI)
 7 Cameroon (CMR)
 8 Austria (AUT)
 9 France (FRA)
10 South Africa (RSA)
11 Saudi Arabia (KSA)
12 Denmark (DEN)
13 Spain (ESP)
14 Nigeria (NGA)
15 Paraguay (PAR)   21 Germany (GER)
16 Bulgaria (BGR)   22 United States (USA)
17 Netherlands (HOL)   23 Yugoslavia (YUG)
18 Belgium (BEL)   24 Iran (IRN)
19 Republic of Korea (KOR) 25 Romania (ROM)
20 Mexico (MEX)   26 Colombia (COL)

PREVIOUS WINNERS OF THE WORLD CUP
Brazil • Italy • West Germany • Uruguay • Argentina • England

27 England (ENG)
28 Tunisia (TUN)
29 Argentina (ARG)
30 Japan (JPN)
31 Jamaica (JAM)
32 Croatia (HRV)

THE COLD WAR

"Even during the Cold War, American "sports diplomats" were received warmly, in the Soviet Union. I was one of such sports envoys," Whitfield recalled. "We found acceptance, love and understanding from the Russians, and in all nations we went simply for the sake of sports."

"C'est beau un monde qui joue" as the French rightly put it, isn't the world that plays a beautiful one? No doubt, people who don't fight, but play together are strong, joyous and full of life.

Competing, winning and losing, sportsmanly and in family spirit and yet continuing in friendship, love, and understanding, all add up to make the world soccer family the greatest bond of its type. Players, trainers, fans, sports administrators and sponsors have all contributed in no small measure to sustain one of the most important relationships on earth – the soccer family.

The 1998 World Cup Squad of Yugoslavia.

CHAPTER THREE

SPONSORS' SUCCESS STORY

THE FINANCIERS

Where would we be without sponsors? "Sponsors and commercial partners provide the funds and some of the resources we need to organize and stage the World Championships," Mr. Jacques Lambert, Managing Director of the French Organising Committee (CFO) of the 1998 World Cup Championships, told journalists in Paris on March 10. "Sponsors are instrumental in making this event happen. They make it possible," Mr. Lambert said. "They are our main backers. We'd never have been able to finance the tournament without the support of the sponsors and the marketing partners. No. Never," he emphasized at the news conference held on March 10, 1998 at the Paris Hotel le Meridien to mark the end of a FIFA workshop for all the 32 teams in the finals of the World Cup competition.

The multilingual President of FIFA, Mr. Joseph S. Blatter, who speaks English, French and Italian fluently, in addition to Swiss German, agreed with Mr. Lambert's views and commended the sponsors and marketing partners for the great role they play in making the World Cup tournaments possible. The seminar brought together all the coaches, national soccer associations' chairmen and officials of the 32 nations for two days of deliberations on plans for the XVI World Cup Championship.

The pronouncements of both Messrs. Lambert and Blatter underscore the indispensable role sponsors and marketing partners play in helping to organize and stage the World Cup championships! Sponsors provide the money, equipment, and services needed to organize the tournament from the planning stage to the end of the tournament.

One good turn really deserves another. How true for the sponsors and marketing partners of the World Cup Championships! Their support of worthy causes like the World Cup Championships and other sporting events and indeed their investment in the lives of the youth and physical fitness of men and women around the world, have turned out to be good for their businesses as well as the welfare of the people they serve.

COMMERCIAL PARTNERS

FIFA and the French Organising Committee work with 45 commercial partners, whose role in marketing, provision of needed equipment and financing the World Cup tournament is described by the French Organising Committee as "crucial." CFO chief executive, Mr. Lambert, pats the marketing affiliates on the back, saying in an interview in Paris, that "our working relationship with the commercial partners is good."

THE STATE

The role of the State in ensuring the success of arrangements and preparations for the World Cup is as important as those of the commercial partners, the CFO and FIFA. For instance, as far back as March 15, 1993, the French Government had put in place the World Cup Interdepartmental Delegation, which is answerable to the Prime Minister. The Minister of Youths and Sports heads the vital body, whose duties, among others, include the coordination of the necessary processes and facilitation of relations between the State and the World Cup Organising Committee. It is also the responsibility of the interdepartmental body to install public amenities and oversee the implementation of World Cup related projects to be co-financed by the State and the private sector. French Youth and Sports Minister Marie-George Buffet has steadfastly continued this good job, which was begun in 1993 under the able leadership of Frederique Bredin, Sports Minister at that time .

CATEGORIES

The French Organising Committee describes its marketing program as "an amazing success." Four categories of commercial partners work with the CFO and FIFA. They are the Official Sponsors, which are twelve in number, and eight Official Suppliers, nine Official Products and Services Providers and 16 Equipment Suppliers.

The national team of Scotland, billed to challenge crown holders, the fabulous Brazilians, in the opening game at Stade de France in Saint-Denis

SPORTING GOODS COMPANIES

Manufacturers and marketing companies of sporting goods, including soccer balls, boots, jerseys, sweat suits and knee and elbow protectors and other equipment are virtually becoming sponsors of the 32 teams, sharing the burden of supply of needed kits and finance with the National Football Associations and Governments worldwide.

PERMANENT STATUS

This list of Official Sponsors of the World Cup Championships changes slightly from one tournament year to another. Some new names are added to the list, while some continue their sponsorship. Other companies do not bid for membership of the elite club in a succeeding tournament, after being sponsors of a previous one. However, some companies like Coca-Cola, seem to retain permanent membership in the much-coveted club.

Mr. Ben Deutsch, Public Relations Manager of Coca-Cola's Worldwide Sports and Presence Properties, said in an interview, "Coca-Cola has a rich, nearly 70-year tradition of supporting football (soccer), dating back to the first World Cup in 1930."

That sponsorship has endured from one tournament to another through the XV edition of the championships to France '98 and almost certainly beyond. The grass withers, flowers bloom and fade, but Coca-Cola is always there for and with the game, its players, and its fans in-season and out-of-season. Players, officials, and spectators seem to love and enjoy the products of Coca-Cola too.

Coca-Cola seems determined to continue this partnership with FIFA, the Local Organising Committees and the fans, for Mr. Deutsch said, "...the World Cup is very important to The Coca-Cola Company and we put a significant portion of our marketing funds and resources against the sponsorship ... to enhance the fans' experience of the event."

Mr. Deutsch emphasized that "Coca-Cola supports football at every level of the game, from grassroots programs to the FIFA World Cup - the pinnacle of international competition."

THE COCA-COLA COMPANY

The Coca-Cola Company remains one of the greatest architects of the world soccer family, building and extending the brotherhood to nearly 200 nations worldwide. Coca-Cola has convincingly and consistently demonstrated its love for and commitment to the global soccer family in various ways. For example, on January 30, 1998, FIFA announced the Coca-Cola decision to extend by eight years its sponsorship of the World Cup Soccer Championships through the first tournament in the 21st century to the XVIII edition of the championships in the year 2006.

Logo: Coca-Cola Worldwide Sports

EFFICACY

M. Douglas Ivester, Chairman and Chief Executive of The Coca-Cola Company, greeted the eight-year agreement with FIFA saying,"the global popularity of football makes it a natural fit for Coca-Cola. It is a partnership we have enjoyed and shared with fans for decades."

The Coca-Cola chief also acknowledged and drew the attention of the world to the efficacy of sports in breaking down the walls of partition between people of different races and ethnic origins, for he noted, "Football is the world's game, a common ground that connects people of different races, origins and cultures throughout the globe … This agreement reinforces our long-term commitment to football and its tremendously passionate fans around the world," Mr. Ivester said.

Outgoing FIFA president Dr. Joao Havelange paid tribute to Coca-Cola for the company's sponsorship and commitment to the worthy cause of global soccer and the satisfaction of its teeming followers. "FIFA is greatly indebted to Coca-Cola for the support it has given not only to the World Cup," Dr. Havelange said, "but also to our grassroots program such as the FIFA/Coca-Cola World Youth Championship."

ISL Marketing, a leading sports marketing company in Lucerne, Switzerland which serves as the marketing agency for FIFA and brokered the agreement, spoke in glowingly laudable terms about the role of The Coca-Cola Company as a sponsor of the World Cup Championship. The Managing Director of ISL, Heinz Schurtenberger, remarked that, "Coca-Cola is an exemplary partner and a true advocate for football."

"It is uniquely qualified to help FIFA continue its mission of promoting the sport to ensure that people in all corners of the globe can enjoy this great game," Schurtenberger said of the agreement and the relationship between FIFA and Coca-Cola which has spanned more than 68 years, dating back to the maiden World Cup soccer joust in 1930. The World Cup soccer family has continued to wax stronger and larger. Indications are that this trend will endure for a long time. Soccer fans love their game passionately and the family is not lacking in charity.

DREAM TEAM

Coca-Cola's long-term commitment and support of soccer and its global family does not end with the World Cup Championship for men. It also includes the Women's World Cup Soccer Championship billed to be held in the United States of America in 1999 and the FIFA U-17 tournament in New Zealand and the World Youth Soccer Championships slated for 1999 in Nigeria, the West African nation that took the soccer world by storm in 1996 with a superlative performance that wrested the coveted Olympic Games' gold medals in the soccer event, triumphing over much fancied Hungary, Japan, Mexico, Brazil and Argentina.

In a game, the amazing coach of Brazil, Mario Zagallo described as "incredible," the Nigerian Dream Team had trailed the Brazilians 1-3 at the interval, but like the proverbial phoenix from the ashes, the Nigerian Super Eagles rose to the challenge, scoring twice to tie the game 3-3 at full time. In the ensuing extra time, the Eagles won the ding-dong match 4-3 before going on to stun Argentina 3-2 in the finals for the gold medals.

OFFICIALLY LICENSED PRODUCTS

ISL Marketing holds the world-wide rights in the area of licensed products. Sony, via its subsidiary company SWC (Sony World Cup), bought these rights for FRANCE 98. The French Organising Committee received a lump-sum payment for the deal.

There is also the official World Cup Village Program – a public relations initiative described as "the largest ever mounted in Europe". It is managed and marketed by the French Organising Committee. The World Cup Final on 12 July 1998 will constitute the biggest public relations operation in the world when nearly 20,000 guests will be received at the Stade de France hospitality village. There will also be a massive sale of officially licensed products at the ten venues in the host cities, including refreshments.

In November 1995, the French Postal Service, La Poste, began offering a series of official "ready-to-post" items, including a range of philatelic products specially designed for stamp-collectors and World Cup lovers! The highlight of the series was the issue of a stamp with a picture of the official France '98 mascot, Footix. Even official coins are also being minted in Paris as part of the program. Its popularity grows with each passing week and it has become become a part of tomorrow's history.

XVI WORLD CUP COMMERCIAL AFFILIATES

THE OFFICIAL SPONSORS

Adidas	*JVC*
Anheuser-Busch	*MasterCard*
Canon	*McDonald's*
Coca-Cola	*Opel*
Fujifilm	*Philips*
Gillette	*Snickers*

THE OFFICIAL SUPPLIERS

Crédit Agricole	*Official Bank of the 1998 World Cup*
Danone	*Official Dairy Products of the 1998 World Cup*
EDS	*Official Supplier of Information Technology to the World Cup*
France Télécom	*Official Telecommunications Operator of the 1998 World Cup*
Hewlett-Packard	*Official Supplier of Computer Equipment to the 1998 World Cup*
La Poste	*Official Mail Carrier of the 1998 World Cup*
Manpower	*Official Temporary Work Network of the 1998 World Cup*
Sybase	*Official Software Supplier to the 1998 World Cup*

OFFICIAL PRODUCTS AND SERVICES

Air France	*Official Airline*
American Power Coversion	*Official Power Protection*
CPW / Nestlé Céréales	*Official Cereals*
Cyanamid	*Official Crop Protection*
La Française des jeux	*Official Lottery*
Lavazza	*Official Coffee*
LG	*Official Electrical Appliances*
Michelin	*Official Tyre*
Total	*Official Petrol*

EQUIPMENT SUPPLIERS

Accor	*Hotel trade*
Algeco	*Modular design and chemical waste disposal*
Arjo-Wiggins	*Paper and paper distribution*
Bosch	*Portable electric tools*
Caterpillar	*Energy backup, air conditioning and air freshening*
Doublet	*Decoration, signage*
Frisquet	*Boilers*
France Secours	*Medical assistance*
Generale Location	*Furnishings and temporary structures*
Geodis	*Logistical organisation*
Guilbert	*Distribution of liquid petroleum gas*
Lafarge	*Building equipment*
Primagaz	*Distribution of liquid petroleum gas*
RATP	*Transport*
SNCF	*Passenger rail transport*
Yves Saint Laurent	*Ready-to-wear designer clothes for men & women*

SPORTING GOODS COMPANIES

Listed are some manufacturers and marketers of balls, boots, jerseys, goalkeepers' gloves, goal nets, shin pads, sports bags and warm-up suits that support some of the World Cup teams and contribute to the overall development of the game around the world.

Nike	Mitre
Adidas	Diadora
Reebok	Arrow
Russell	Pony
Puma	Harrods
Kappa	New Balance
Loto	American Soccer Company
Umbro	Mizuno
Soccer Select	Sondico
Asics	Quaser
Spalding	Unisport
Makita	Wilson

CHAPTER FOUR

THE BIRTH OF THE CHAMPIONSHIPS

A NEW BRIDGE TO ALL NATIONS

The inauguration of a global governing body for soccer early in the 20th century laid the foundation for the eventual birth of the World Cup soccer championship. The Federation of International Football Associations (FIFA) was founded in Paris, France, on May 2, 1904 at a meeting of national soccer associations of France, Belgium, Denmark, The Netherlands, Spain, Sweden, and Switzerland.

FIFA is the brainchild of the French journalist Robert Guerin, whose conviction that soccer needed an international authority to administer the games universal rules and nuture its growth, initiated moves that led to the birth of the global soccer governing body. Guerin, the soccer patriarch, was deservedly elected the first president in Paris in 1904, at the inaugural meeting of the global soccer governing body attended by nationals of seven nations.

A new dawn broke for soccer on May 26, 1928, when the Congress of the International Federation of Football Associations meeting in Amsterdam, the Netherlands took an epoch-making decision to organize a global competition "open to all teams representing the affiliated national associations." The decision was taken by a vote of 23 to 5. True to the innovative and pioneering spirit of the French, whose Baron Pierre de Coubertin in 1896 revived and modernized the Olympic Games, begun by the sports-loving ancient Greeks in 900 B.C., the World Cup soccer tournament is also the brainchild of Frenchmen.

Jules Rimet, President of FIFA from 1921 and Secretary-General Henri Delaunay, both French nationals, midwived the birth of the championships. At the FIFA Congress in 1928, the house voted to approve the proposal for commencing a global soccer tournament. But it was not until 1929 at Barcelona, Spain that FIFA finally decided to go ahead with plans for staging the World Cup championship.

THE JULES RIMET ERA

There were only 13 entrants for the maiden World Cup tournament. All the 13 nations played in the final stages of the championship. Apparently due to time constraint and the few number of nations willing to participate, preliminary rounds were not played to eliminate contenders and prune down the number of participants in the championship as is the case now.

World Cup championships
Results from 1930-1970

URUGUAY 1930
The Maiden
World Cup Tournament

Group 1

Argentina 6 Mexico 3
Argentina 3 Chile 1
Argentina 1 France 0
Chile 3 Mexico 0
Chile 1 France 0
France 4 Mexico 1

Group 2

Brazil 4 Bolivia 0
Yugoslavia 4 Bolivia 0
Yugoslavia 2 Brazil 1

Group 3

Romania 3 Peru 1
Uruguay 1 Peru 0
Uruguay 4 Romania 0

Group 4

Paraguay 1 Belgium 0
USA 3 Belgium 0
USA 3 Paraguay 0

Semifinals

Argentina 6 USA 1
Uruguay 6 Yugoslavia 1

The Final

Uruguay 4, Argentina 2
Winner: **Uruguay**

ITALY 1934
II WORLD CUP

First Round

Austria 3 France 2
Czechoslovakia 2 Romania 1
Germany 5 Belgium 2
Hungary 4 Egypt 2
Italy 7 USA 1
Sweden 3 Argentina 2
Switzerland 3 Netherlands 2

Second Round

Austria 2 Hungary 1
Czechoslovakia 3 Switzerland 2
Germany 2 Sweden 1
Italy 1 Spain 0

Semifinals

Czechoslovakia 3 Germany 1
Italy 1 Austria 0

3rd Place Match

Germany 3 Austria 2

Championship Game

Italy 2 Czechoslovakia 1
Champion: **Italy**

FRANCE 1938
III WORLD CUP

First Round

Brazil 6 Poland 5
Cuba 2 Romania 1
Czechoslovakia 3 Netherlands 0
France 3 Belgium 1
Hungary 6 Dutch East Indies 0
Italy 2 Norway 1
Switzerland 4 Germany 2,

Second Round

Brazil 2 Czechoslovakia 1
Hungary 2 Switzerland 0
Sweden 8 Cuba 0

Semifinals

Hungary 5 Sweden 1
Italy 2 Brazil 1

3rd Place Game

Brazil 4 Sweden 2

The Final Game

Italy 4 Hungary 2
Champions: **Italy**

BRAZIL 1950
IV WORLD CUP

Group 1

Brazil 4 Mexico 0
Yugoslavia 3 Switzerland 0
Brazil 2 Switzerland 2
Brazil 2 Yugoslavia 0
Switzerland 2 Mexico 1
Yugoslavia 4 Mexico 1

Group 2

Chile 5 USA 2
England 2 Chile 0
Spain 3 USA 1
Spain 2 Chile 0
Spain 1 England 0
USA 1 England 0

Group 3

Italy 2 Paraguay 0
Sweden 3 Italy 2
Sweden 2 Paraguay 2

Group 4

Uruguay 8 Bolivia 0

The Last Six

Brazil 7 Sweden 1
Brazil 6 Spain 1
Sweden 3 Spain 1
Uruguay 3 Sweden 2
Uruguay 2 Spain 2
Uruguay 2 Brazil 1
Winners: **Uruguay**

SWITZERLAND 1954
V WORLD CUP

Group 1

Brazil 5 Mexico 0
Brazil 1 Yugoslavia 1
France 3 Mexico 2
Yugoslavia 1 France 0

Group 2

Hungary 9 Korea 0
Hungary 8 West Germany 3
Turkey 7 Korea 0
West Germany 4 Turkey 1
West Germany 7 Turkey 2
   (playoff)

Group 3

Austria 5 Czechoslovakia 0
Austria 1 Scotland 0
Uruguay 7 Scotland 0
Uruguay 2 Czechoslovakia 0

Group 4

England 4 Belgium 4
England 2 Switzerland 0
Italy 4 Belgium 1
Switzerland 4 Italy 1 (playoff)
Switzerland 2 Italy 1

Quarterfinals

Austria 7 Switzerland 5
Hungary 4 Brazil 2
Uruguay 4 England 2
West Germany 2 Yugoslavia 0

Semifinals

Hungary 4 Uruguay 2
West Germany 6 Austria 1

3rd Place Game

Austria 3 Uruguay 1

Championship Game

West Germany 3 Hungary 2
   Winners: **West Germany**

SWEDEN 1958
VI WORLD CUP

Group 1

Argentina 3 Northern Ireland 1
Czechoslovakia 6 Argentina 1
N. Ireland 1 Czechoslovakia 0
West Germany 3 Argentina 1
West Germany 2 Czechoslovakia 2
West Germany 2 Northern Ireland 2
Northern Ireland 2 Czechoslovakia 1

Group 2

France 7 Paraguay 3
France 2 Scotland 1
Paraguay 3 Scotland 2
Yugoslavia 3 France 2
Yugoslavia 3 Paraguay 3
Yugoslavia 1 Scotland 1

Group 3

Hungary 4 Mexico 0
Hungary 1 Wales 1
Sweden 3 Mexico 0
Sweden 2 Hungary 1
Sweden 0 Wales 0
Wales 2 Hungary 1 (playoff)
Wales 1 Mexico 1

Group 4

Brazil 3 Austria 0
Brazil 2 USSR 0
England 2 Austria 2
England 2 USSR 2
England 0 Brazil 0
USSR 2 Austria 0
USSR 1 England 0 (playoff)

Quarterfinals

Brazil 1 Wales 0
France 4 Northern Ireland 0
Sweden 2 USSR 0
West Germany 1 Yugoslavia 0

Semifinals
Brazil 5 France 2
Sweden 3 West Germany 1

3rd Place Game
France 6 West Germany 3

THE FINAL
Brazil 5 Sweden 2
   Champion: **Brazil**

CHILE 1962
VII WORLD CUP

Group 1
Uruguay 2 Colombia 1
USSR 4 Colombia 4
USSR 2 Uruguay 1
USSR 2 Yugoslavia 0
Yugoslavia 5 Colombia 0
Yugoslavia 3 Uruguay 1

Group 2
Chile 3 Switzerland 1
Chile 2 Italy 0
Italy 3 Switzerland 0
West Germany 2 Switzerland 1
West Germany 2 Chile 0
West Germany 0 Italy 0

Group 3
Brazil 2 Mexico 0
Brazil 2 Spain 1
Brazil 0 Czechoslovakia 0
Czechoslovakia 1 Spain 0
Mexico 3 Czechoslovakia 1
Spain 1 Mexico 0

Group 4
Argentina 1 Bulgaria 0
Argentina 0 Hungary 0
England 3 Argentina 1
England 0 Bulgaria 0
Hungary 6 Bulgaria 1
Hungary 2 England 1

Quarterfinals
Brazil 3 England 1
Chile 2 USSR 1
Czechoslovakia 1 Hungary 0
Yugoslavia 1 West Germany 0

Semifinals
Brazil 4 Chile 2
Czechoslovakia 3 Yugoslavia 1

3rd Place Game
Chile 1 Yugoslavia 0

CHAMPIONSHIP GAME
Brazil 3 Czechoslovakia 1
   Champion: **Brazil**

ENGLAND 1966
VIII WORLD CUP

Group 1
England 2 France 0
England 2 Mexico 0
England 0 Uruguay 0
Franc 1 Mexico 1
Uruguay 2 France 1
Uruguay 0 Mexico 0

Group 2
Argentina 2 Spain 1
Argentina 2 Switzerland 0
Argentina 0 West Germany 0
Spain 2 Switzerland 1
West Germany 5 Switzerland 0
West Germany 2 Spain 1

Group 3

Brazil 2 Bulgaria 0
Hungary 3 Brazil 1
Hungary 3 Bulgaria 1
Portugal 3 Brazil 1
Portugal 3 Bulgaria 0
Portugal 3 Hungary 1

Group 4

Chile 1 North Korea 1
Italy 2 Chile 0
North Korea 1 Italy 0
USSR 3 North Korea 0
USSR 2 Chile 1
USSR 1 Italy 0

Quarterfinals

England 1 Argentina 0
Portugal 5 North Korea 3
USSR 2 Hungary 1
West Germany 4 Uruguay 0

Semifinals

England 2 Portugal 1
West Germany 2 USSR 1

Final Decider

England 4 West Germany 2
Winner: **England**

MEXICO 1970
IX WORLD CUP

Group 1

Belgium 3 El Salvador 0
Mexico 4 El Salvador 0
Mexico 1 Belgium 0
Mexico 0 USSR 0
USSR 4 Belgium 1
USSR 2 El Salvador 0

Group 2

Israel 1 Sweden 1
Israel 0 Italy 0
Italy 1 Sweden 0
Sweden 1 Uruguay 0
Uruguay 2 Israel 0
Uruguay 0 Italy 0

Group 3

Brazil 4 Czechoslovakia 1
Brazil 3 Romania 2
Brazil 1 England 0
England 1 Czechoslovakia 0
England 1 Romania 0
Romania 2 Czechoslovakia 1

Group 4

Bulgaria 1 Morocco 1
Peru 3 Bulgaria 2
Peru 3 Morocco 0
West Germany 5 Bulgaria 2
West Germany 3 Peru 1
West Germany 2 Morocco 1

Quarterfinals

Brazil 4 Peru 2
Italy 4 Mexico 1
Uruguay 1 USSR 0
West Germany 3 England 2

Semifinals

Brazil 3 Uruguay 1
Italy 4 West Germany 3

3rd Place Duel

West Germany 1 Uruguay 0

The Battle Royale

Brazil 4 Italy 1
Champion: **Brazil**

 **CHAPTER FIVE**

THE FIRST WORLD CUP TOURNAMENT

A NEW BRIDGE TO ALL NATIONS

Soccer's global governing body, the Federation of International Football Associations (FIFA), set the stage in 1928 for the first World Cup soccer championship to be held at a later date, in 1930. At its Congress in Amsterdam, The Netherlands, FIFA decided to hold a global soccer tournament that would draw participants from all nations.

FIFA reaffirmed its decision at Barcelona, Spain in 1929 and intensified arrangements for staging the maiden World Cup tournament. Until the inception of the World Cup soccer championship, the soccer event of the Olympic Games was the pinnacle of global soccer competitions.

Rather auspiciously, it was Uruguay, a South American nation, which did not belong to the fold of the seven founding fathers, that was given the pride of place to host the first World Cup championship. Again, the gesture to Uruguay was another testimony to the magnanimity of Jules Rimet and Henri Delaunay. The other founding fathers were not quite as accommodating and gracious. That triggered a partial boycott of the tournament by some European countries.

Uruguay was the leading soccer nation on earth at the time it sought and won the bid to host the maiden World Cup tourney. The South American nation had won the prestigious soccer event of the Olympic Games in 1924 and 1928. The fact of their reign as soccer kings of the Olympic world reinforced their bid. But that was not all. The Uruguayans were glaringly more determined to win the bid than any other country. Their bid was the most attractive.

MAGNA CARTA

The year 1930 marked the 100th year of the Uruguayan Constitutional Oath, which enshrined the principles of democracy, rule of law and respect of the people for the new Magna Carta. The choice of the summer of 1930 to bid and host the first World Cup soccer championship was all the more significant for the people of Uruguay. It also commemorated the centennial anniversary of the independence of Uruguay as a nation. Although Uruguay earned her independence on August 25, 1825, it was not until July 18, 1830 that the country adopted her independence Constitution. "The first Constitution is the second legal pronouncement of Uruguay as an independent country," explained Eduardo Rosenbrock of the Embassy of Uruguay in Washington, D.C.

The Uruguayan government and people prepared their bid and worked conscientiously to host the world. Dr. Raul Jude, President of "Associacion Uruguaya de Futbol" – the Uruguayan Soccer Association, Enrique Buero and Hector Rivadavia Gomez were at the vanguard of the efforts and arrangements with the blessings of the government.

GLORIOUS DAYS

Their efforts paid off copiously at last. Uruguay, the underdogs, turned the tables against much touted European bidders to win the rights to host the first World Cup tournament. The FIFA Congress held at Barcelona, Spain in 1929 awarded the bid to the South American nation. Mr. Buero and Mr. Rivadavia Gomez represented Uruguay at the Barcelona meeting.

Uruguay hosted the tournament, lived up to its billing as the Olympic Games soccer title holders of the 1920's and won the championship in grand style. The various games of the tournament were played at the Estadio Centenario, Parque Central and the now defunct stadium, Estadio de Peniarol in Pocitos. Uruguayans revel until this day in their "decadas de gloria" – years of (soccer) glory and have built the 'Museo del Futbol' – a Montevideo museum of soccer - in memory of their great feat in 1930 and other soccer exploits in the Olympic Games and the 1950 World Cup title which they also won.

1998 World Cup championship
Early results, facts and figures

First goal scored by: Cesar Sampaio of BRAZIL in the 4th minute
First goalkeeper to concede a goal: Jim Leighton of SCOTLAND
First own goal: by Tom Boyd of SCOTLAND
First penalty committed by: Cesar Sampaio of BRAZIL
First penalty scored by: John Collins of SCOTLAND, 38th minute
First team to defeat a top seed: NIGERIA
First seeded team to lose a game: SPAIN
First red card victim: Ha Seok-ju of SOUTH KOREA
First Star to emerge: Moustafa El Hadji of MOROCCO

Games and Scorers

Brazil 2   Scotland 1 *(80,000 spectators)*
   Cesar Sampaio [Brazil]
   Tom Boyd [Scotland] Own goal deflected into his net
   John Collins [Scotland] Penalty
Venue: Stade de France, Saint-Denis on June 10, 1998
Referee: Jose-Mario Garcia-Aranda [Spain]

Cameroon 1   Austria 1
   Pierre Njanka [Cameroon]
   Toni Polster [Austria]
Venue: Stadium Municipal, Toulose
Referee: Epifanio Gonzalez Chavez [Paraguay]

Chile 2   Italy 2
   Marcelo Salas (2 goals) [Chile]
   Christian Vieri [Italy]
   Roberto Baggio (penalty kick) [Italy]
Venue: Stade Lescure Bordeaux
Referee: Lucian Bouchardeau [Niger]

Morocco 2   Norway 2
   Moustafa El Hadji [Morocco] 38th minute
   Abdeljibil Hadda [Morocco] 45th minute
   Youssef Chippo [Morocco] Own goal deflected into his net
      in the 45th minute
   Dan Eggen 62nd minute [Norway]

Nigeria 3   Spain 2
   Mutiu Adepoju, Garba Lawal, Sunday Oliseh [Nigeria]
   Fernando Hierro, Raul Gonzalez [Spain]

France 3   South Africa 0
   Chris Dugarry, Pierre Issa, Thierry Henry [France]

Mexico 3   South Korea 1
   Ricardo Pelaez, Luis Hernandez (2 goals) [Mexico]
   Ha Seok-ju [South Korea]

1998 World Cup championship

Italy 2   Chile 2
Scotland 1   Norway 1
Bulgaria 0   Paraguay 0
Denmark 1   Saudi Arabia 0
Belgium 0   Netherlands 0
Yugoslavia 1   Iran 0
Croatia 3   Jamaica 1
Argentina 1   Japan 0
England 2   Tunisia 0
Romania 1   Colombia 0
Germany 2   USA 0

USA 1994
XV WORLD CUP

Group A

USA 1 Switzerland 1
Colombia 1 Romania 3
Romania 1 Switzerland 4
USA 2 Colombia 1
USA 0 Romania 1
Switzerland 0 Colombia 2

Group B

Cameroon 2 Sweden 2
Brazil 2 Russia 0
Brazil 3 Cameroon 0
Sweden 3 Russia 1
Brazil 1 Sweden 1
Russia 6 Cameroon 1

Group C

Germany 1 Bolivia 0
Spain 2 South Korea 2
Germany 1 Spain 1
South Korea 0 Bolivia 0
Germany 3 South Korea 2
Bolivia 1 Spain 3

Group D

Argentina 4 Greece 0
Nigeria 3 Bulgaria 0
Argentina 2 Nigeria 1
Bulgaria 4 Greece 0
Argentina 0 Bulgaria 2
Greece 0 Nigeria 2

Group E

Italy 0 Ireland Republic 1
Norway 1 Mexico 0
Italy 1 Norway 0
Mexico 2 Ireland Republic 1
Italy 1 Mexico 1
Ireland Republic 0 Norway 0

Group F

Belgium 1 Morocco 0
Netherlands 2 Saudi Arabia 1
Belgium 1 Netherlands 0
Saudi Arabia 2 Morocco 1
Belgium 0 Saudi Arabia 1
Morocco 1 Netherlands 2

Second Round

Germany 3 Belgium 2
Spain 3 Switzerland 0
Sweden 3 Saudi Arabia 1
Romania 3 Argentina 2
Holland 2 Ireland 0
Brazil 1 United States 0
Italy 2 Nigeria 1
Mexico 1 Bulgaria 1
(Bulgaria won 3-1 in shoot-out)

Quarterfinals

Italy 2 Spain 1
Brazil 3 Netherlands 2
Bulgaria 2 Germany 1
Sweden 2 Romania 2
(Sweden won 5-4 on penalties)

Semifinals

Italy 2 Bulgaria 1
Brazil 1 Sweden 0

USA 1994 World Cup

A	W	L	T	GE	GA	Pts
Romania	2	1	0	5	5	6
Switzerland	1	1	1	5	4	4
United States	1	1	1	3	3	4
Colombia	1	2	0	4	5	3
B						
Brazil	2	0	1	6	1	7
Sweden	1	0	2	6	4	5
Russia	1	2	0	7	6	3
Cameroon	0	2	1	3	11	1
C						
Germany	2	0	1	5	3	7
Spain	1	0	2	6	4	5
South Korea	0	1	2	4	5	2
Bolivia	0	2	1	1	4	1
D						
Nigeria	2	1	0	6	2	6
Bulgaria	2	1	0	6	3	6
Argentina	2	1	0	6	3	6
Greece	0	3	0	0	10	0
E						
Mexico	1	1	1	3	3	4
Ireland	1	1	1	2	2	4
Italy	1	1	1	2	2	4
Norway	1	1	1	1	1	4
F						
Netherlands	2	1	0	4	3	6
Saudi Arabia	2	1	0	4	3	6
Belgium	2	1	0	2	1	6
Morocco	0	3	0	2	4	0

Third Place

Sweden 4 Bulgaria 0

Championship Game

Brazil 0 Italy 0
  Winners: **Brazil**
  (3-2 on Penalties)

ITALIA 1990
XIV WORLD CUP

Group A

Austria 2 USA 1
Czechoslovakia 5 USA 1
Czechoslovakia 1 Austria 0
Italy 2 Czechoslovakia 0
Italy 1 Austria 0
Italy 1 USA 0

Group B

Argentina 2 USSR 0
Argentina 1 Romania 1
Cameroon 2 Romania 1
Cameroon 1 Argentina 0
Romania 2 USSR 0
USSR 4 Cameroon 0

Group C

Brazil 2 Sweden 1
Brazil 1 Costa Rica 0
Brazil 1 Scotland 0
Costa Rica 2 Sweden 1
Costa Rica 1 Scotland 0
Scotland 2 Sweden 1

Group D

Colombia 2 UAE 0
Colombia 1 West Germany 1
West Germany 5 UAE 1
West Germany 4 Yugoslavia 1
Yugoslavia 4 UAE 1
Yugoslavia 1 Colombia 0

Group E

Belgium 3 Uruguay 1
Belgium 2 South Korea 0
Spain 3 South Korea 1
Spain 2 Belgium 1
Spain 0 Uruguay 0
Uruguay 1 South Korea 0

Group F

Egypt 1 Netherlands 1
Egypt 0 Ireland 0
England 1 Ireland 1
England 1 Egypt 0
England 0 Netherlands 0
Netherlands 1 Ireland 1

Round of 16

Argentina 1 Brazil 0
Cameroon 2 Colombia 1
Czechoslovakia 4 Costa Rica 1
England 1 Belgium 0
Ireland 5 Romania 4
Italy 2 Uruguay 0
West Germany 2 Netherlands 1
Yugoslavia 2 Spain 1

Quarterfinals

Argentina 3 Yugoslavia 2
England 3 Cameroon 2
Italy 1 Ireland 0
West Germany 1 Czechoslovakia 0

Semifinals

Argentina 4 Italy 3
West Germany 4 England 3

3rd Place Duel

Italy 2 England 1

Championship Game

West Germany 1 Argentina 0
  Winners: **West Germany**

MEXICO 1986
XIII WORLD CUP

Group A

Argentina 3 South Korea 1
Argentina 2 Bulgaria 0
Argentina 1 Italy 1
Bulgaria 1 Italy 1
Bulgaria 1 South Korea 1
Italy 3 South Korea 2

Group B

Mexico 1 Iraq 0
Belgium 2 Paraguay 2
Belgium 2 Iraq 1
Mexico 2 Belgium 1
Mexico 1 Paraguay 1
Paraguay 1 Iraq 0

Group C

France 3 Hungary 0
France 1 Canada 0
France 1 USSR 1
Hungary 2 Canada 0
USSR 6 Hungary 0
USSR 2 Canada 0

Group D

Algeria 1 Northern Ireland 1
Brazil 3 Northern Ireland 0
Brazil 1 Algeria 0
Brazil 1 Spain 0
Spain 3 Algeria 0
Spain 2 Northern Ireland 1

Group E

Denmark 6 Uruguay 1
Denmark 2 West Germany 0
Denmark 1 Scotland 0
Scotland 0 Uruguay 0
West Germany 2 Scotland 1
West Germany 1 Uruguay 1

Group F

England 3 Poland 0
England 0 Morocco 0
Morocco 3 Portugal 1
Morocco 0 Poland 0
Poland 1 Portugal 0
Portugal 1 England 0

Round of 16

Argentina 1 Uruguay 0
Belgium 4 USSR 3
Brazil 4 Poland 0
England 3 Paraguay 0
France 2 Italy 0
Mexico 2 Bulgaria 0
Spain 5 Denmark 1
West Germany 1 Morocco 0

Quarterfinals

Argentina 2 England 1
Belgium 5 Spain 4
France 4 Brazil 3
West Germany 4 Mexico 1

Semifinals

Argentina 2 Belgium 0
West Germany 2 France 0

3rd Place Battle

France 4 Belgium 2

The Grand Finale

Argentina 3 West Germany 2
Trophy Taker: **Argentina**

ESPAÑA 1982
XII WORLD CUP

Group 1

Cameroon 1 Italy 1
Cameroon 0 Peru 0
Cameroon 0 Poland 0
Italy 1 Peru 1

Italy 0 Poland 0
Poland 5 Peru 1

Group 2

Algeria 3 Chile 2
Algeria 2 West Germany 1
Austria 2 Algeria 0
Austria 1 Chile 0
West Germany 4 Chile 1
West Germany 1 Austria 0

Group 3

Argentina 4 Hungary 1
Argentina 2 El Salvador 0
Belgium 1 Argentina 0
Belgium 1 El Salvador 0
Belgium 1 Hungary 1
Hungary 10 El Salvador 1

Group 4

Czechoslovakia 1 France 1
Czechoslovakia 1 Kuwait 1
England 3 France 1
England 2 Czechoslovakia 0
England 1 Kuwait 0
France 4 Kuwait 1

Group 5

Honduras 1 Northern Ireland 1
Honduras 1 Spain 1
Northern Ireland 1 Spain 0
Northern Ireland 0 Yugoslavia 0
Spain 2 Yugoslavia 1
Yugoslavia 1 Honduras 0

Group 6

Brazil 4 Scotland 1
Brazil 4 New Zealand 0
Brazil 2 USSR 1
Scotland 5 New Zealand 2
Scotland 2 USSR 2
USSR 3 New Zealand 0

Semifinal Group A

Poland 3 Belgium 0
Poland 0 USSR 0
USSR 1 Belgium 0
 USSR Successful

Semifinal Group B

England 0 Spain 0
England 0 West Germany 0
West Germany 2 Spain 1
 West Germany Qualified

Semifinal Group C

Brazil 3 Argentina 1
Italy 3 Brazil 2
Italy 2 Argentina 1
 Italy Triumphed

Semifinal Group D

Austria 2 Northern Ireland 2
France 4 Northern Ireland 1
France 1 Austria 0
 France Qualified

Semifinals

Italy 2 Poland 0
West Germany 5 France 4

3rd Place Game

Poland 3 France 2

Final

Italy 3 West Germany 1
 Champions: **Italy**

ARGENTINA 1978
XI WORLD CUP

Group 1

Argentina 2 France 1
Argentina 2 Hungary 1
France 3 Hungary 1
Italy 3 Hungary 1
Italy 2 France 1
Italy 1 Argentina 0
 Qualifiers: Italy, Argentina

Group 2

Poland 3 Mexico 1
Poland 1 Tunisia 0
Poland 0 West Germnay 0
Tunisia 3 Mexico 1
Tunisia 0 West Germany 0
West Germany 6 Mexico 0
Qualifiers: Poland, West Germany

Group 3

Austria 2 Spain 1
Austria 1 Sweden 0
Brazil 1 Austria 0
Brazil 1 Sweden 1
Brazil 0 Spain 0
Spain 1 Sweden 0
   Qualifiers: Austria, Brazil

Group 4

Iran 1 Scotland 1
Netherlands 3 Iran 0
Netherlands 0 Peru 0
Peru 4 Iran 1
Peru 3 Scotland 1
Scotland 3 Netherlands 2
   Qualifiers: Peru, Netherlands

Semifinal Group A

Austria 3 West Germany 2
Italy 1 Austria 0
Italy 0 West Germany 0
Netherlands 5 Austria 1
Netherlands 2 West Germany 2
Netherlands 2 Italy 1
   Winner: Netherlands
   Runner-up: Italy

Semifinal Group B

Argentina 6 Peru 0
Argentina 2 Poland 0
Argentina 0 Brazil 0
Brazil 3 Peru 0

Brazil 3 Poland 1
Poland 1 Peru 0
   Winner: Argentina
   Runner-up: Brazil

3rd Place Game

Brazil 2 Italy 1

Final

Argentina 3 Netherlands 1 (o/t)
   Champion: **Argentina**

GERMANY 1974
X WORLD CUP

Group 1

East Germany 1 West Germany 0
Australia 0 Chile 0
East Germany 2 Australia 0
East Germany 1 Chile 1
West Germany 3 Australia 0
West Germany 1 Chile 0

Group 2

Brazil 3 Zaire 0
Brazil 0 Scotland 0
Brazil 0 Yugoslavia 0
Scotland 2 Zaire 0
Scotland 1 Yugoslavia 1
Yugoslavia 9 Zaire 0

Group 3

Bulgaria 1 Uruguay 1
Netherlands 4 Bulgaria 1
Netherlands 2 Uruguay 0
Netherlands 0 Sweden 0
Sweden 3 Uruguay 0
Sweden 0 Bulgaria 0

Group 4

Argentina 4 Haiti 1
Argentina 1 Italy 1
Italy 3 Haiti 1
Poland 7 Haiti 0

Poland 3 Argentina 2
Poland 2 Italy 1

Semifinal Group A

Argentina 1 East Germany 1
Brazil 2 Argentina 1
Brazil 1 East Germany 0
Netherlands 4 Argentina 0
Netherlands 2 Brazil 0
Netherlands 2 East Germany 0
    Winner: Netherlands
    Runner-up: Brazil

Semifinal Group B

Poland 2 Yugoslavia 1
Poland 1 Sweden 0
Sweden 2 Yugoslavia 1
West Germany 4 Sweden 2
West Germany 2 Yugoslavia 0
West Germany 1 Poland 0
    Winner: West Germany
    Runner-up: Poland

3rd Place Match

Poland 1 Brazil 0

Championship Game

West Germany 2 Netherlands 1
    Year's Best: **West Germany**

 **CHAPTER SIX**

FANS AND THE FUN

THE CHEERS AND THE BOOS

The number of spectators, who watch the games at the various venues has risen phenomenally since the first World Cup tournament was played in Uruguay in 1930. So also has the global television audience. For instance, in the premier tournament 547,308 spectators watched the 18 matches played in 1930. But by 1994, when the XV FIFA World Cup tournament was played in the United States of America, the fans who were present at the terraces to see the 52 matches increased to a total of 3,587,538 spectators, while the cumulative global television audience was a whopping 30 billion fans. Though more people listen to radio commentators of sporting events in the developing world, these global figures do not include listeners of World Cup games' commentaries on the radio.

CLINTON'S MESSAGE

President Bill Clinton of the United States, in his welcome message to players, officials, and fans during USA '94, acknowledged the World Cup Soccer Championship as "the world's largest sporting event, drawing more than three million spectators." "The United States," President Clinton said, was "extremely gratified to have the opportunity to host the World Cup for the first time ever."

"I am delighted" Clinton said, "to extend a special welcome to all those who have traveled from around the globe to witness and to participate in this exciting event." The U.S. President wished all the 24 finalists "good luck" and expressed the hope that all players and fans would "enjoy an exciting and memorable World Cup tournament."

Lustily cheering fans in the background during a tense moment in the 1-0 triumph of Brazil over Sweden in the 1994 World Cup Semifinal.
Photo: Allsport Photography USA, Inc. / Shaun Botterill

World Cup Tournaments From 1930 - 1998
Record of fans attendance and global television viewers

Year	Host Nation (No. of games)	Fans Present	Results
1930	Uruguay (18)	547,308	Uruguay 4, Argentina 2
1934	Italy (17)	408,602	Italy 2, Czechoslovakia 1
1938	France (18)	483,000	Italy 4, Hungary 2
1950	Brazil (22)	1,337,000	Uruguay 2, Brazil 1
1954	Switzerland (26)	943,000	West Germany 3, Hungary 2
1958	Sweden (35)	868,000	Brazil 5, Sweden 2
1962	Chile (32)	896,336	Brazil 3, Czechoslovakia 1
1966	England (32)	1,614,677	England 4, West Germany 2
1970	Mexico (32)	1,673,975	Brazil 4, Italy 1
1974	Germany (38)	1,774,022	West Germany 2, Netherlands 1
1978	Argentina (38)	1,747,210	Argentina 3, Netherlands 1
1982	Spain (52)	2,073,723	Italy 3, West Germany 1
1986	Mexico (52)	2,373,051	Argentina 3, West Germany 2
1990	Italy (52)	2,517,348	West Germany 1, Argentina 0
1994	USA (52)	3,587,538	Brazil 3, Italy 2

Brazil won by penalties after a scoreless draw

USA '94

Number of games played by all 24 teams = 52
Spectators at the bleachers to watch 24 games = 3,587,538
Estimated cumulative audience worldwide = 30 billion viewers

FRANCE '98

Number of matches played by all the 32 teams = 64
Estimated cumulative television audience worldwide = 37 billion
Estimated television viewers for the title game = 1.7 billion

Footnote: The television audience given for USA '94 and France '98 are cumulative figures, meaning that the total number is gotten from successive addition of the viewers of each and all the games played in the series. It is therefore no wonder that the World Cup cumulative television audience is more than the population of the world, which is estimated at 5,582,000,000.

Fans gather every four years in millions. Far away from home, but feeling very much at home. But for some spectators, especially those of the host nation, the convocation could be right at their backyard or in their home town. They look forward to it with avid interest.

Why do they converge? For the World Cup tournament; for the fun and excitement it brings. For the soccer fireworks and wizardry that come with it. The memorable moments, the great goals and the incredible upsets are among the attractions.

The brand of football served here is the finest, more fluid than any served elsewhere on earth. It is the most flowery type of soccer. It is a delight to watch. These are just some of the goodies about the World Cup tourney that draws people from around the world to see it or watch on television or listen to commentaries of the matches on radio.

Players, especially the ball jugglers, are a bundle of delight to watch. They lighten the stands and seats with their soccer wizardry and dribbles. They bring a lot of excitement to the spectators and television audience. Fans come with the side attraction and the extra touch.

SUPPORTERS' CLUB

Every nation in the finals of the World Cup Championship is followed by a multitude of faithful supporters. These supporters are usually partisan fans, whose duty is to lustily cheer on their national teams and players into greater heights and scoring. They are fond of such choruses as "Give us more goals. All we are saying, give us more goals." The songs vary from one nation to the other, but the message is always clear. It is intended to spur the players into action and score more goals.

Fans of opposing nations sometimes indulge in booing the play of each other, especially when blunders are made in vital areas of the field. Though this is not always the case, such negative reactions are aimed at demoralizing the opponent, so that your team can gain the upper hand. Blind patriotism and partisanship are displayed all too often, but are to be expected in a competition in which the pride, mood and prestige of nations are at stake.

Spectators pay thousands of dollars and travel thousands of miles to and from the host nation to join other fans in the soccer fiesta. Some nations provide financial support for members of their supporters' clubs. Others don't and the spectators have to defray the cost of the trip

EXCITEMENT

The fan's day starts with thoughts of the game, analysis, and discussions with friends and other spectators. The upcoming game is the fan's prayer and cup of tea. It is the spectator's preoccupation, indeed, his obsession.

Thrills of the game keep fans in a frenzy of excitement. That is not all. The fans even excite one another.

They sleep, dreaming about the impending game. They wake up with thoughts of it in the morning. Then comes the decisive moment. The match is played, won and lost. Elated at the triumph of their team or disappointed at the loss of the side they support, they go to bed with pleasant or haunting memories of the previous game.

Fans display the highest spirit of sportsmanship. They forgive the boos, the antagonism and the rivalry of the previous game. They forget the sorrows of the lost game and share the joy of the won match. "No victor, no vanquished", some broadminded fans would say. "Let's delight at the fluidity, the beauty of the action-packed game," you would hear others say.

They come in thousands. Their approach is jubilant and hilarious. It is an unmistakable sight — a sea of heads and legs. All roads lead to the stadium. Some dressed in their national costumes and others in bizarre clothing, the fans throng into the stadium for a World Cup game, carrying their national flags, banners and sometimes photos of their national stars. Others pull the crowds with their drums and dances. All of this is in the name of the sport they love.

UGLY SIDE OF THE COIN

There is also the ugly side of the coin. The better side does not always win. Sometimes it is the luckier side. The day could be carried by fluke. A flash-in-the-pan performance is what does the trick at times. Despite the magnanimity and high sense of sportsmanship most fans show on the terraces and in front of the television screens and at radio listening points, some fans simply react violently to the sight or news of the loss of their darling team. Stampede, insults, riots, partisan fist fights, and even disaster could ensue. Sometimes the police have to be called in to restore order and escort players and the referee away from angry and vengeful supporters of a defeated team.

SIDE ATTRACTIONS

Several side attractions are being planned to complement the main show — the World Cup tournament. Perhaps the greatest of them is by The Coca-Cola Company which plans to bring 1,600 young soccer fans to France '98. One thousand of the youths would serve as ceremonial flag bearers, 500 as official ball kids and 60 budding stars will play in pre-game contests before the kickoff of some World Cup matches. "It is an unprecedented chance to be part of the world's largest single sport event in a unique and memorable way," Scott McCune, Vice President and Director, Worldwide Sports of The Coca-Cola Company, said. Mr. McCune expressed the belief that the makers of the world's most popular soft drinks would "bring soccer fans around the globe so close to the 1998 World Cup, they'll be able to touch it, literally." Fans can look forward with avid interest to a special treat, the like of which is rare to come by. This and many more are the great expectations of fun, soccer at its best and excitement that attract fans to the greatest sporting event under the sun — the World Cup Soccer Championship!

Players and officials of the Saudi World Cup squad

 **CHAPTER SEVEN**

TICKETS AND QUOTAS

A BONE OF CONTENTION

Allotment of tickets among the constituent bodies of FIFA, the Local Organising Committees and their affiliates has always been a delicate issue. The provision, sale and purchase of World Cup tickets are no less thorny issues. Never before has there been so much hullaballoo over the rationing, provision, sale, and purchase of tickets as that triggered by the XVI edition of the World Cup Championships!

Global demand for France '98 tickets is estimated at 20 million, but FIFA and the French Organising Committee can supply only 2.5 million tickets. Mr. Joseph Blatter, President of FIFA, couldn't have described the situation in a better way, when at a Paris news conference, he likened the shortfall between the demand for tickets and supply to "a beautiful woman (who) cannot give of herself to every interested man."

The joy of fans is to gain legal entry into the venue of a game and watch at the terraces the proceedings live. This access is made possible with the purchase of a valid ticket and presentation of same to gatekeepers at the turnstile before the beginning of a match. Similarly, a ticket is needed for one to be allowed into the stadium to see a World Cup game from the bleachers. Possession of a valid ticket is usually verified at the gates and permission is given by security personnel to the spectator to go into the terraces to watch the game.

Under the guidelines of the tickets policy formulated for France '98 by the Local Organising Committee and approved by FIFA, actual tickets will not be distributed to their owners until shortly before the start of the World Cup.

"At present, only ticket vouchers, exchangeable for proper tickets, are in circulation," Mr. Andrin Cooper of FIFA's Media Office said in an interview. He expressed the hope that the precautionary measure would "substantially reduce the chances of ticket racketeering and forgery."

Allaying fears of fans that ticket fraud could mar the smooth running of the XVI tournament, Mr. Jacques Lambert, Managing Director of the French Organising Committee, said at a news conference in Paris, "We are prepared to take stern

Jacques Lambert, Managing Director of the French Organising Committee of the 1998 World Cup Tourney.

measures to deter ticket touts and hoarding with the aid of French Security agents, especially in and around the match venues."

THE RATIONING FORMULA

A total of 1.5 million tickets are earmarked for sale to people in France and the French soccer community. This accounts for about 60 percent of all tickets available for sale worldwide. Not only did this rationing formula spark of controversies in Europe, it was also, no doubt, a bone of contention elsewhere in the world. In compliance with the rules and regulations of the global governing body, 20% or .5 million tickets go to FIFA and the national soccer associations affiliated to it.

Altogether about 2.5 million tickets were offered for sale to spectators to watch 64 matches of the XVI World Cup tournament. Half a million of the tickets sold at 150 French Francs, while others had a price tag of 250 French Francs or less. Allocations to the French Organising Committee (CFO) and foreign commercial affiliates were put at 300,000 tickets or 12 percent, while 200,000 tickets or 8% were rationed to officially approved tour operators and ticket agencies located mainly in the 32 nations in the World Cup finals for sale to spectators.

TICKET AGENCIES

Several sports travel companies got FIFA's approval to operate as official ticket agencies. The companies also have capabilities for arranging tours and trips for fans travelling to France for the World Cup tournament. Among the official ticket agencies are: Gullivers Sports Travel, Mike Burton Sports Travel, and Voss & Votava Sportreisen which offer services in several parts of the world, but have a strong presence in Europe. Others operating largely in Europe include Pauwels Travel Bureau and Ken Air Tours. Primesport International serves also as an official ticket agency in several parts of the world.

Omvesa operates as a World Cup ticket agency mainly in South and North America, but also in Spain. Primesport International is another official ticket agency that operates in various parts of the world, including Brazil, Cameroon, Columbia, Mexico, and Saudi Arabia.

The African market for World Cup tickets is dominated by Wagonlit Sports Travel, which in some countries like Nigeria, is represented by Transcap, a travel agency. Sportsworld Fli Afrika - another agency - serves mainly South Africa, and Scottish fans.

JT Travel operates as an official travel agency in Asia, particularly in Japan and Korea, although Japan is also served by Primesport International.

World Cup tickets can also be obtained from Stella Barros Turismo, which operates in Argentina, Chile, and Paraguay. The Rail Europe Group also serves as an official ticket agency in New York.

Enumerated under each Continent are the names of the countries and cities where official ticket agencies are located.

SOUTH AMERICA

ARGENTINA: *Omvesa* - Beunos Aires, Bahia Blanca, Cordoba, Mar de Plata, Mendoza, Rosario, Santa Fé, San Juan, San Miguel de Tucuman; *Primesport International* - Buenos Aires; *Stella Barros Turismo,* in Buenos Aires and Sao Paulo.

BRAZIL: *Omvesa* - in Belem, Belo Horizonte, Brasilia, Curitiba, Fortaleza, Manaus, Natal, Porto Alegre, Portovelho, Rio de Janeiro, Recife, Salvador de Bahia, Sao Paulo; *Primesport International* in Sao Paulo; *Stella Barros Turismo* in Sao Paulo.

CHILE: *Omvesa* in Santiago de Chile; *Primesport International* in Santiago de Chile; *Stella Barros-Turismo* in Santiago de Chile.

COLOMBIA: *Omvesa* in Barranquilla, Cali, Manizales, Medellin, Santa Fé de Bogota; *Primesport International* in Bogota; *Stella Barros Turismo* in Santa Fé De Bogota.

PARAGUAY: *Omvesa* in Asunción; *Stella Barros Turismo* in Asunción.

NORTH AND CENTAL AMERICA

USA: *Gullivers Sports Travel* in Vista, CA; *Omvesa* in Los Angeles, Miami, New York; *Primesport International* in Miami, Beverly Hills, CA; *Rail Europe Group* in New York.

MEXICO: *Gullivers Sports Travel* in Mexico City, *Omvesa* in Guadalajara, Mexico City, Monterrey, Puebla, Tijuana; *Primesport International* in Mexico City.

JAMAICA: *Guillivers Sports Travel* in Mandeville.

AFRICA

CAMEROON: *Primesport International* in Douala; *Wagonlit Sports Travel* in Douala, Yaounde.

MOROCCO: *Wagonlit Sports Travel* in Agadir, Casablanca, Fès, Marrakech, Meknes, Oujda, Rabat, Tanger.

NIGERIA: *Wagonlit Sports Travel* in Kano, Lagos, Port Harcourt.

SOUTH AFRICA: *Sports World Fli Afrika* in Johannesburg; *Wagonlit Sports Travel* in Illovo.

TUNISIA: *Wagonlit Sports Travel* in Tunis.

ASIA

IRAN: *Mike Burton Travel Bureau, Pauwels Travel Bureau, Voss & Votava Sportsreiser, Wagonlit Sports Travel and branches of Crédit Agricole.*

JAPAN: *JT Travel* in Tokyo; *Primesport International* in Tokyo.

SAUDI ARABIA: *Primesport International* in Jeddah.

SOUTH KOREA: *JT Travel* in Seoul.

EUROPE

AUSTRIA: *Gullivers Sports Travel* in Vienna; *Mike Burton Sports Travel* in Vienna; *Voss & Votava Sportreisen* in Vienna.

BELGIUM: *Pauwels Travel Bureau* in Diegem.

BULGARIA: *Mike Burton Sports Travel* in Sofia.

CROATIA; *Gullivers Sports Travel* in Zagreb; *Mike Burton Sports Travel* in Zagreb.

DENMARK: *Gullivers Sports Travel* in Copenhagen; *Mike Burton Sports Travel* in Vejle Rejser.

ENGLAND: *Gullivers Sports Travel* in Gloucestershire; *Ken Air Tours* in London; *Mike Burton Sports Travel* in Gloucester; *Primesports International* in London; *Sportsworld Fli Afrika* in Abingdon.

FRANCE: *Mike Burton Sports Travel* in Paris: *Pauwels Travel Bureau* in Paris; *Voss & Votava Sportreisen* in Strasbourg; *Wagonlit Sports Travel* in Paris.

GERMANY: *Gullivers Sports Travel* in Meerbusch; *Mike Burton Sports Travel* in Germany; *Voss & Votava Sportreisen* in Unna.

ITALY: *Gullivers Sports Travel* in Milan; *Mike Burton Sports Travel* in Milan.

NETHERLANDS: Gullivers Sports Travel in Amsterdam;
   Mike Burton Sports Travel in Rotterdam;
   Pauwels Travel Bureau in Hoofddorp.

NORWAY: *Gullivers Sports Travel* in Grimstao;
   Mike Burton Sports Travel in Norway;
   Voss & Votava Sportreisen in Oslo.

ROMANIA: *Gullivers Sports Travel* in Bucharest.

SPAIN: *Gullivers Sports Travel* in Madrid;
   Mike Burton Sports Travel in Barcelona;
   Omvesa in Madrid; *Voss & Votava Sportreisen* in Madrid.

SCOTLAND: *Guillivers Sports Travel* in Gloucestershire;
   Ken Air Tours in London; *Mike Burton Sports Travel* in
   Gloucester; *Primesport International in London
   (same as ticket agencies in England).*

YUGOSLAVIA: *Voss & Votava Sportreisen* in Belgrade.

 **CHAPTER EIGHT**

SUPERSTARS

THE INIMITABLE

The global championships have featured the most talented players the world has ever produced. Virtually every position of player has been blessed with two or more superstars. There have been and continue to be goalkeepers, defenders and attackers of extraordinary ability.

Midfield aces and schemers have emerged from the World Cup tournaments. The world has also seen goal merchants who struck and scored with geometric precision.

A galaxy of stellar players have adorned World Cup tourneys. Among the greatest of them is Edson Arantes do Nascimento, nicknamed Pele, of Brazil, Gerd Müller, and Franz Beckenbaeur of Germany, Mozambique-born Eusebio da Silva Ferreira of Portugal, Bobby Charlton of England, Dutch aces Johan Cruyff, and Johan Neeskens and Gary Lineker.

Goalkeepers Lev Yashin of the USSR and Dino Zoff, one of the world's longest serving goal tenders of his time and a former captain of Italy, and compatriots Paolo Rossi and Roberto Baggio are among the greatest performers the game has produced. Other superstars include French soccer idols Just Fontaine and Michel Platini, Argentina's Danielle Pasarella, Mario Kempes and Diego Maradona, Roger Milla of Cameroon.

Pele was a rare breed of star, who played soccer with his brain, brawn, head, chest, and laps. He never forgot to fit his thinking cap on the field of play. He knew where to receive or pass the ball. Placing himself always in a vantage position, goal scoring was his second nature. He adorned his career with a very good conduct on and off the field.

French Superstar Michel Platini

WORLD CUP BEST STRIKERS & GOAL MERCHANTS

Pele - *Edson Arantes do Nascimento*	1958, 62, 70	Brazil
Gerd Müller	1970, 74	Germany
Just Fontaine	1958	France
Eusebio da Silva Ferreira	1966	Portugal *(Mozambique-born)*
Sandor Kocsis	1954	Hungary
Teofilo Cubillas	1970, 78	Peru
Geoff Hurst	1966, 70	England
Johan Cruyff	1974	The Netherlands
Gary Lineker	1986	England
Mario Kempes	1978	Argentina
Paolo Rossi	1982	Italy
Diego Maradona	1986, 90, 94	Argentina
Marco van Basten	1990	The Netherlands
Roger Milla	1986, 90, 94	Cameroon
Ronaldo *Best Player of the World '97*	1994,98	Brazil
Zico	1982	Brazil
Socrates	1982	Brazil

STELLAR WINGERS OF WORLD CUP FAME

Garrincha	1958, 62	(L) Brazil
Jairzinho	1970	(R) Brazil
Mario Zagallo	1958, 62	Brazil
Rivelino	1970	(L) Brazil
Gregorz Lato	1974	Poland
Emmanuel Amuneke	1994	Nigeria
Finidi George	1994,98	Nigeria

MIDFIELD ACES and MOST VERSATILE PLAYERS

Franz Beckenbaeur	1966, 70,74	West Germany
Bobby Charlton	1966, 70	England
Gerson	1970	Brazil
Gunter Netzer	1970	West Germany
Johan Neekens	1974, 78	The Netherlands
Michel Platini	1978, 82, 86	France
Kaz Deyna	1974	Poland
Sunday Oliseh	1994, 98	Nigeria

MOST ENTERTAINING PLAYERS OF THE WORLD CUP

Tostao	1970	Brazil
Gerson	1970	Brazil
Everaldo	1970	Brazil
Johan Cruyff	1974	The Netherlands
Zico	1982	Brazil
Austin Okocha	1994, 98	Nigeria

STOPPERS AND SWEEPERS

Bobby Moore	1966, 70	England
Danielle Passarella	1978, 82	Argentina
Antonio Cabrini	1970	Italy
Paolo Maldini	1990	Italy
Paul Breitner	1974	West Germany
Taribo West	1998	Nigeria

AGILE GOALKEEPERS

Lev Yashin	1958	USSR
Sepp Maier	1974	West Germany
Dino Zoff	1982	Italy
Gordon Banks	1966	England
Jan Tomaszewski	1974	Poland
Thomas Nkono	1990	Cameroon

WORLD CUP TEAM MANAGERS
VICTORIOUS COACHES

Coach	Country	Year
Carlos Alberto Parreira	Brazil	1994
Franz Beckenbauer	West Germany	1990
Carlos Bilardo	Argentina	1986
Enzo Bearzot	Italy	1982
Cesar Luis Menotti	Argentina	1978
Helmut Schoen	West Germany	1974
Mario Zagallo	Brazil	1970
Sir Alf Ramsey	England	1966
Aimore Moreira	Brazil	1962
Vincente Feola	Brazil	1958
Josef Herberger	West Germany	1954
Juan Lopez	Uruguay	1950
Vittorio Pozzo	Italy	1938
Vittorio Pozzo	Italy	1934
Alberto Supicci	Uruguay	1930

SUPER STARS
HIGHEST GOAL SCORERS IN EACH TOURNEY

Year	No. of Goals	Player	Country
1994	6	Oleg Salenko	Russia
1994	6	Hristo Stoichkov	Bulgaria
1990	6	Salvatore Schillaci	Italy
1986	6	Gary Lineker	England
1982	6	Paolo Rossi	Italy
1978	6	Mario Kempes	Argentina
1974	7	Gregorz Lato	Poland
1970	10	Gerd Müller	Germany
1966	9	Eusebio	Portugal
1962	5	Drazen Jerkovic	Yugoslavia
1958	13	Just Fontaine	France
1954	11	Sandor Kocsis	Hungary
1950	9	Ademir	Brazil
1938	8	Leonidas da Silva	Brazil
1934	4	Edmund Conen	Germany
1934	4	Angelo Schiavio	Italy
1934	4	Oldrich Nejedly	Czechoslovakia
1930	8	Guillermo Stabile	Argentina

NATIONS THAT HAVE QUALIFIED FOR THE
WORLD CUP SO FAR

A total of 70 countries played in the World Cup Competition during the 68 years of the Championships in the 20th Century, some appearing over 10 times and others only once. Listed are the nations that the superstars propelled into the final stages of the World Cup from 1930 to 1998:

Country	No. of Times	Years participated
Brazil	16	1930,34,38,50,54,58,62,66,70,74,78,82,86,90,94,98
Italy	14	1934,38,50,54,62,66,70,74,78,82,86,90,94,98
Argentina	12	1930,34,58,62,66,74,78,82,86,90,94,98
Mexico	11	1930,50,54,58,62,66,70,78,86,94,98
West Germany	10	1954,58,62,66,70,74,78,82,86,90
France	10	1930,34,38,54,58,66,78,82,86,98
England	10	1950,54,58,62,66,70,82,86,90,98
Belgium	9	1934,38,54,70,82,86,90,94,98
Hungary	9	1934,38,54,58,62,66,78,82,86
Spain	9	1934,50,62,66,78,82,90,94,98
Sweden	9	1934,38,50,58,70,74,78,90,94
Uruguay	9	1930,50,54,62,66,70,74,86,90
Yugoslavia	9	1930,50,54,58,62,74,82,90,98
Czechoslovakia	7	1934,38,58,62,70,82,90
USSR	7	1958,62,66,70,82,86,90
Austria	7	1934,54,58,78,82,90,98
Bulgaria	7	1962,66,70,74,82,94,98
Chile	7	1930,50,62,66,74,82,98
Romania	7	1930,34,38,70,90,94,98
Scotland	7	1958,74,78,82,86,90,98
Switzerland	7	1934,38,50,54,62,66,94
USA	6	1930,34,50,90,94,98
The Netherlands	6	1934,74,78,90,94,98
Poland	5	1938,74,78,82,86
United Germany	4	1934,38,94,98
Cameroon	4	1982,90,94,98
Columbia	4	1962,90,94,98
Paraguay	4	1930,50,86,98
Peru	4	1930,70,78,82
Morocco	4	1970,86,94,98
South Korea	4	1986,90,94,98
Bolivia	3	1930,50,94
Norway	3	1938,94,98
Algeria	2	1982,86

Denmark	2	1986,98	El Salvador	1	1982
Egypt	2	1934,90	Greece	1	1994
Iran	2	1978,98	Haiti	1	1974
Nigeria	2	1994,98	Honduras	1	1982
Portugal	2	1966,86	Iraq	1	1986
Saudi Arabia	2	1994,98	Israel	1	1970
Tunisia	2	1978,98	Jamaica	1	1998
Australia	1	1974	Japan	1	1998
Canada	1	1986	Kuwait	1	1982
Costa Rica	1	1990	North Korea	1	1966
Croatia	1	1998	Russia	1	1994
Cuba	1	1938	Turkey	1	1954
Dutch East Indies	1	1938	UAE	1	1990
East Germany	1	1974	Zaire	1	1974

The 10 Commandments of Soccer

1 Play to win
2 Play fair
3 Observe the laws of the game
4 Respect opponents, teammates, referees, officials and spectators
5 Accept defeat with dignity
6 Promote the interest of football
7 Reject corruption, drugs, racism, violence and other dangers to our sport
8 Help others to resist corrupting pressures
9 Denounce those who attempt to discredit our sport
10 Reverence those who defend football's good reputation

Most of the superstars, including Pele, Eusebio and Platini, have not only distinguished themselves and adorned their careers with their exceptional performances on the field of play, but also with their good conduct off the pitch. They faithfully kept the laws of the game and its commandments.

 **CHAPTER NINE**

THE MEMORABLE MOMENTS

SOCCER WIZARDRY, GOALS, MISSES AND UPSETS

World Cup Soccer is not without its joyous and sad moments. The championships have been full of great and memorable hours. Every tournament has featured some of the most outstanding displays of soccer wizardry. Uncanny scoring ability, goals scored with geometric precision, terrible misses and upsets have all combined to make the World Cup championships the most thrilling and unforgettable sporting event under the sun.

The great moments are not created by the famous players only. Such instances sometimes create the stars and bring a hitherto unknown player into the limelight.

AFRICAN WONDER BOY

The 1966 World Cup, for example, was replete with such moments. It brought into fame Eusebio da Silva Ferreira, the inimitable African boy from Mozambique, whose four amazing goals for Portugal turned the tables against North Korea. The Asians were leading 3-0, before Eusebio's glorious moments came. It was an unforgettable show of soccer artistry and uncanny scoring ability! Eusebio netted four goals in quick succession and was instrumental in scoring the fifth in a timely rally that saved the day 5-3 for Portugal.

Eusebio outshone even the mighty Pele, in the clash of titans between Brazil and Portugal, in which Eusebio turned on a sparkling performance from his centre forward position to earn Portugal a 3-1 triumph over Brazil, the defending champions in the 1966 World Cup, having won the championship in 1962. Eusebio confounded the world with his soccer artistry and unimaginable goals.

Korean players jubilate after scoring a crucial goal in the 1994 World Cup
Photo: Allsport Photography (USA) Inc. / Ben Radford

GREAT GOALS

The 1970 World Cup tournament starred some of the finest players ever to play in the championships. Most of the aces were fielded by Brazil, who paraded the inimitable midfield trio of Everaldo, Gerson and Tostao in addition to Pele, and the amazing scorer and right winger Jairzinho, who cut a niche for himself with his golden goal against the legendary goalkeeper Gordon Banks of England. Great goals also came from West Germany's Gerd Müller who hit home some of the most acclaimed goals of that tournament, in which he emerged as the highest scorer.

MISSES

The World Cup championships have witnessed some terrible misses and lost opportunities. Hungary, Czechoslovakia and the Netherlands, two-time losers at the finals of the World Cup, appear to have lost more opportunities in the tournament than any other nation. That a nation could get to the finals and end up as runners-up in a competition in which about 200 nations quadrennially lock horns from the qualifying stage is by no means a small feat, though.

One of the most baffling misses was in the 1970 World Cup when England's attack frittered a golden opportunity in Brazil's danger zone to find the net for the much needed equaliser. The miss was in the front of a porous Brazilian rearguard and an easily assailable cover provided by goalkeeper Felix, who was weak in both the air and on the ground.

UPSETS

Perhaps the greatest upset ever caused in the series was the United States 1-0 pip of England in the 1950 World Cup championship. The United States had entered the pitch as underdogs, but proved the bookmakers wrong, emerging as the dark horse of that year's tournament in Brazil, that was eventually won by Uruguay.

The 1966 World Cup witnessed a jolt and debacle for Italy, who lost 0-1 to North Korea, whose spirited campaign in the tournament had given them a 3-0 lead over Portugal in another match before the irrepressible Eusebio propelled the Portuguese to victory.

Cameroon's 1-0 defeat of Argentina in their Group B first round match of the 1990 World Cup championships was another bombshell that shook the soccer world. The feat brought Roger Milla and some of his teammates, including the agile goalkeeper Thomas Nkono, into the limelight.

GERMAN MIRACLE

West Germany's rebound from an 0-1 first round defeat in the hands of East Germany and subsequent win of the World Cup in 1974 against all odds was a memorable feat. The West Germans had entered the pitch for the championship game against the Netherlands as the underdogs, even on their own soil. The bookmakers and other observers had good reasons for betting on the Dutch to win.

The Netherlands had dethroned defending Champions, Brazil 2-0, walloped Argentina 4-0 after trouncing Bulgaria 4-1 and Uruguay 2-0. Incredible performance! With such a record, was it not safe to predict a walkover for the Netherlands in the finals? Absolutely yes! But the West Germans proved the bookmakers wrong in one of the most memorable finals of the World Cup.

Led by the indomitable, Franz Beckenbauer, the Germans rebounded from a first-minute penalty goal to turn back the spirited performance of the Dutch. West Germany won 2-1 at last. What an unforgettable game; thanks to the agile goalie Sepp Maier, Beckenbauer and Berti Vogts!

CHINESE FANS

Just imagine for a moment your compatriot mounting the victor's podium, standing head and shoulders above the two others, who placed second and third, with a gold medal laced around his neck and you will get a clearer picture of the dream of World Cup soccer fans!

The preceding scenario explains the agony of millions of soccer fans in China, the world's largest nation, when it failed to qualify for the 1998 World Cup tournament – the fifth time in succession since its futile effort to play in the 1982 World Cup championship in Spain. October 31, 1997 was literally a day of mourning for the Chinese people. On that day, Qatar, a small Persian Gulf nation of 665,000 people, defeated China and dashed the hopes of its 1.2 billion people for making their debut in the World Cup soccer championship. Chinese fans reacted sharply to the "denting of our national pride" with a massive protest on the streets.

In the city of Dalian, no less than 5,000 demonstrators besieged the streets chanting their disappointment and shock at the poor performance of the national players, their coach and officials of the Soccer Association.

The irate fans pressed for the disbanding of the Chinese Soccer Association and the resignation of the national coach. The leadership of the Chinese Soccer Federation was very responsive to the outrage and tendered an apology to the nation for its poor performance. In the letter of remorse, the Chinese Soccer Association said "Our self-blame and regret are deep. We don't know what to say at this moment other than sorry". The leadership of the Soccer Association assured the Chinese people that their "criticisms and sincere teachings are engraved on our bones and imprinted in our hearts". The mood and reaction of the Chinese fans reflected the importance nations attach to the World Cup championship. It may not be a do-or-die affair, but qualifying to play in the World Cup tournament is the dream of all soccer-loving nations. It is a matter of national prestige.

 **CHAPTER TEN**

A TITANIC STRIDE

FROM ONE MILESTONE TO ANOTHER

It has been a giant and steady step forward from the kickoff of ancient soccer in China during the Han dynasty, all the way through the inception of the modern game in England in 1863, the inauguration of FIFA in 1904 and the World Cup championships in 1930. World soccer has developed from infancy to adulthood, from years of uncertainty to an era of stability and prosperity. Indeed it has been a titanic stride for the game. Yes, a step from one milestone to another for soccer – the sport the great Edson Arantes do Nascimento, known the world over as Pele, styled "the beautiful game."

THE EXPONENTS

Claims and debates over the origin of soccer are older than the modern game and as fiery as a keenly contested, ding-dong match. However, China's claim is buttressed with more abundant evidence and, by any yardstick, more credible and convincing than any provided by other claimants. For sure, China is the oldest continually existing civilization in the world. Besides, there are ample and clear records that an ancient ball game in the semblance of modern soccer was played in China. "It was probably invented during the reign of Liu Ao, whose official name was Ch'eng-ti" said Liu Zhengrong of the Chinese Embassy in Washington, D.C. Although several records refer to the Chinese game as Tsu-Chu, Mr. Liu believes it was called Zu Oui, meaning football in Mandarin - the standard Chinese language.

Kemari - the second form of soccer played under the sun - is believed to have its origin in Japan, established as a nation in the year 660 B.C. under the reign of Jimmu. This form of ancient soccer of Japanese fame was believed to have been played around

650 A.D. during the reign of Emperor Koutoku, according to Miss Makiko Uemura of the Embassy of Japan in Washington, D.C. "The word kemari means traditional sport," she said.

The Egyptians of hieroglyphics fame are believed to have had their hands and feet in the origin of soccer. Although there are indications that some type of soccer might have been played in the ancient land, the accounts are still hazy about the form their game took or what role they played in developing the ancient game.

In their characteristic love for sports the Greeks, known and extolled as exponents of the Olympic Games, also added their innovative minds to the growth and spread of soccer. Their brand of soccer was called Episkyros. "The game was especially popular in Sparta, a famous Greek city ," said Connie Mourtoupalas of the Embassy of Greece in Washington, D.C.

The ancient Romans also played a ball game called Harpastum. The Moroccans, Tunisians and native North Americans are also believed to have played some early type of ball game in the semblance of modern soccer.

Credit for organising the game into association football and developing the rules to regulate the conduct of the game, its players and officials incontrovertibly goes to the English people, whose pioneering efforts culminated in the formation of association football and the making of the first set of laws to regulate the game in 1863. It is no wonder, therefore, that until now the International Football Association Board (IFAB), which makes the laws of soccer, comprises one national of England, Scotland, Wales, and Ireland with one vote each. The four other voting members of the IFAB are drawn from the Federation of International Football Associations with its headquarters in Zurich, Switzerland.

The game has known even better days since 1863. Then came the FIFA era from 1904 and onwards to the inception of the World Cup soccer championships in 1930.

A NEW ERA

The World Cup Championships even survived the bumps of the World Wars and is triumphing through the 20th into the 21st century. By the turn of the century, 16 tournaments would have been successfully staged.

From Montevideo, Uruguay to Saint-Denis, France, from the first World Cup to the XVI edition, except for some intermittent setbacks, it has been one success story after the other. The tournament has grown by leaps and bounds. From a humble start in 1930, the indefatigable and concerted efforts of its organizers, players and sponsors have vaulted the championships to enviable heights. FIFA, the local organising committees and the commercial partners are waxing stronger with every passing year and every tournament. The future of world soccer is bright and secured.

68 YEARS OF SOCCER FIESTA

The direction in which soccer and the World Cup Championships is heading seems to be clear: higher standards of play, fitter and fairer players, more entertainment and more fun. More value for the spectator's money for tickets and better deals for players and the financiers of the industry. Safer and more secure stadia. Fairer and more just standards of officiating. FIFA seems to have charted a definite course it wants to follow. All for the good of the game and the common good.

ADORNING THE GAME

Soccer is an industry in several countries including Great Britain and Italy. Yet it is far more than that. The industry has arisen because it was a widespread activity long before modern mass efforts made it famous. Soccer is not just a pasttime or recreation. For some of its ardent lovers and disciples it is a religion. It is an entertainment. It brings delight to the hearts of the men and women, the boys and girls who watch it. It is a thing of beauty - a joy for the spectators and the viewers and listeners to the commentaries on radio.

The beauty of it all is that the governing body of soccer in the world, FIFA, is not leaving any stone unturned to ensure improved and higher standards of play, fitness, and fairness and to reduce injuries to the barest minimum. The game is getting better and better. And this, at a time, when rough tactics, brutality and indiscipline are incapacitating and threatening the lives of players in some other games.

Soccer is not a game that encourages actions which present potential danger to the health of players. It does not require so many protective devices to prevent lifelong injuries to the players.

At least, testing the ability of these protective devices is not the primary purpose of the game as in the American version of 'football' or rugby.

Vicious tackles, violent collisions, exchanges of blows and fighting are virtually taking the beauty out of football, rugby, baseball, hockey and even basketball. Fans who pay so much to watch these sports no longer get the best value for their money. The situation is reminiscent of the days of the Roman gladiators.

Mr. Joseph Blatter

Beautifying the game

Newly elected FIFA President, Mr. Joseph S. Blatter, who has served FIFA and the world of soccer since 1975, is one of the greatest builders of a smoother, better and cleaner road for soccer. He has worked so hard to make the game even more beautiful. Mr. Blatter refers to soccer as "the world's most popular game with an ingenious balance between simplicity and sophistication." "Efforts," he insists, must be made relentlessly to "defend and improve the game that it may continue to retain the pride of place it has earned among all arms of sport." In fervent pursuit of his goals of adorning the game, Mr. Blatter announced on March 10, 1998 in Paris, additions to laws of the game intended to ensure clean play and fairness.

NEW LAW

One of such moves is the much-awaited clamp-down on unfair tackles. The International Football Association Board at its 112th meeting in Paris in March 1998 enacted an addition to Law XII stating that "a tackle from behind which endangers the safety of an opponent must be sanctioned as serious foul play." Referees are allowed under the law to punish cases of serious infringement with the imposition of a red card or outright expulsion of the offending player from the field.

The new addition to the laws of soccer, intended to rid the game of acts of rough play and brutality, will be applied during the 1998 World Cup competition, but takes global effect from July 1, 1998. It came in the wake of advice from the FIFA Technical and Sports Medical Committees amidst the increasing number of injuries sustained by players, viciously tackled from behind. The law was enacted at a time FIFA is making an effort to stamp out rough play and violent tactics from the game and move towards attaining its goal of ensuring "the beauty of the game."

There are seventeen laws of soccer, dwelling on and regulating various aspects of the game, including:

1. **The Field of Play**
2. **The Ball**
3. **The Number of Players**
4. **The Players' Equipment**
5. **The Referee**
6. **The Linesman or Assistant Referee**
7. **Duration of the Match**
8. **The Start and Resumption of Play**
9. **The Ball In and Out of Play**
10. **The Method of Scoring**
11. **Offside**
12. **Fouls and Misconduct**
13. **Free Kicks**
14. **The Penalty Kick**
15. **The Throw-in**
16. **The Goal Kick**
17. **The Corner Kick**

PELE'S LAW

Racism in sports -- for which South Africa was, for years, ostracized from the global sporting community -- did not die with apartheid in Nelson Mandela's country. The malady still rears its ugly head all around the world in various forms.

For example, a British Government Task Force on soccer found on March 30, 1998 in London that apartheid and discrimination based on considerations other than competence and merit still existed within local soccer clubs, although racism had "diminished at the professional level." The Task Force, which submitted its report to British Sports Minister Tony Banks, warned that "racist (soccer) teams would be banned" from playing on government owned playgrounds. Is there any better way to deal with the monster? The British Government must be commended for taking the bull by the horns.

Pele has also started a crusade in his native Brazil to sanitize the game and improve the conduct of its players, club owners and administrators. In a bill he initiated, while in office as Sports Minister of Brazil, Pele sought to "end slavery and corruption in soccer." "Lei Pele," as the law is called, is a watershed, a titanic stride, indeed, in the development of soccer.

DREAM OF SPECTATORS

The dream of every soccer spectator is to root for his nation at the World Cup soccer championship. For soccer fans in some nations it is a long dream that does not easily come to pass. They may have to wait for years, in some cases decades, for their national players to steer the ship of their dream into the port of realization. It takes hard work, discipline, strategy, grooming and sharpening of their skills through regular practice. It is not just the dream of soccer fans. It is also the yearning of government leaders and people of all countries to see their nations play in the World Cup and have their national flag waved. What a joy it brings to watch your nation win laurels and have your national anthem played and greeted at the end with a thunderous ovation!

THE WOMEN'S WORLD CUP

The increasing interest that women have shown in soccer around the world is another testimony to the relentless efforts the FIFA leadership has made to improve the game and make it more attractive. FIFA broke new grounds in November 1991, when it inaugurated and staged the first Women's World Cup soccer championship in China.

The second edition of the tournament was played in 1995. This was followed by the introduction of the women's soccer event at the Centennial Olympic Games in Atlanta in 1996. The fairer sex may not be interested in playing a brutal and violent game. This accounts, perhaps, for the increasing interest women have shown in the fairer and more "beautiful" game FIFA is striving for. The third edition of the Women's World Cup championship will be hosted in the summer of 1999 by the United States of America.

CHAPTER ELEVEN

2002 TWIN HOSTS: JAPAN AND KOREA

A NEW DAWN

The International Federation of Football Associations (FIFA), the governing body of soccer in the world, broke new grounds on May 31, 1996. FIFA decided on that day to award, for the first time, to two nations the rights to host the first World Cup to be staged in the 21st century. The rare opportunity went to Japan and Korea. The decision followed a keenly contested bid.

Joao Havelange, the outgoing president of FIFA, made the epoch-making announcement in Zurich, Switzerland six years before the tournament kicks off.

It is the first time the championship will be held on Asian soil. For both the people and governments of Korea and Japan, it was not just a welcome verdict, it was shared joy. Perhaps, FIFA's decision meant more to the Koreans. For one, they started the race for the bid as underdogs against the Japanese

Did the announcement herald the beginning of a new era? Or was it simply a way of solving the difficult problem that the attractive offers of both Japan and Korea presented to FIFA? FIFA has not told the world that the World Cup championship may continue to be co-hosted by two nations after 2002. The indications are that such possibilities exist and may be applied where and when necessary.

Both nations entered the race as strong contenders. Japan had hosted the Olympic Games in 1964 and Korea in 1988. Each nation has in place stadia and other facilities that are needed to host the championships and people from around the world who converge at the cities of the host nation to watch. Although the Koreans were no pushovers, the Japanese apparently had an edge early in their campaign to win the bid.

JAPAN

Japan mounted one of the strongest and most concerted campaigns ever by any nation seeking to land the World Cup bid. The issue of the bid unified even opposing sides of the Japanese Parliament, the Diet, whose members acted in one accord.

Japanese Prime Minister, Ryutaro Hashimoto (second from left) and former South Korean President Kim Young Sam (second from right) mark the historic co-host arrangement for the 2002 World Cup with an exchange of soccer balls bearing the signatures of the two leaders
Photo: Korean Overseas Information Service, Seoul

PARLIAMENTARY EFFORT

The Land of the Rising Sun, as Japan is sometimes styled, left no one in doubt as to its determination to wrest the bid from other contenders. The Parliamentary Action Committee for the World Cup 2002 was put in place under the chairmanship of the then Prime Minister Kiichi Miyazawa. Comprising 339 members from all the parties, the Diet Action Committee on the World Cup 2002 was widely regarded as "the largest and strongest multi-party committee in Japan's political history!"

In November 1989, the Japanese Football Association made public its intention to contest for the bid. This was followed in October 1991 by the inauguration of the World Cup Japan 2002 Bidding Committee.

On February 21, 1995, the Japanese cabinet adopted a resolution reaffirming the government's support for the nation's bid to host the tournament. The Parliamentary Action Committee was to marshal, among other things, a concerted effort of the government and the private sector towards providing the facilities and atmosphere that would win the bid for Japan.

Japan submitted a glaringly attractive and convincing bid to FIFA. Among other goodies and credentials Japan flaunted before FIFA were the nation's successful organisation and hosting of the Olympic Games and the FIFA World Youth Championship and well-built stadia with state-of-the-art technology. Other credentials the Japanese Bidding Committee presented to FIFA for consideration were the nation's "stable economy, punctual and extensive transportation system", political stability, public safety and order. Japan also drew the attention of the soccer world it seeks to host to its 6,231 hotels and 90,130 inns as well as the hospitality of its people. It was an irresistible offer.

KOREA

Still basking in the glory of its successful hosting of the 1988 Olympic Games, Korea was indeed a formidable opponent in the race for the bid to host the first World Cup tournament in Asia.

Korea mounted a great campaign and presented a very attractive bid. Although the race for the bid had the staunch support of the soccer loving Korean people and the then President Kim Young Sam, credit for bringing the World Cup partly to Korea, in a manner reminiscent of the successful bid for the 1988 Olympic Games, goes to Chung Mong-Joon, president of the Korean Football Association (KFA). Chung's father, Chung Ju-yung, a Hyundai Company chief, is believed to be the architect of Korea's wrest of the 1988 Olympic bid.

The energetic Chung was at the vanguard of efforts to win the bid for his country, globe-trotting and lobbying FIFA executive council members to award the rights to Korea. An insider of FIFA and vice president of soccer's global governing body, Chung certainly knew what to do and he played his cards circumspectly.

His efforts paid off when the issue of whether to award the championship to Japan or Korea reportedly divided the world's number one football house. The compromise reached brought shared joy to Japan and Korea. For Chung it was a reward for hard work, a triumph for his untiring travail for his nation, and a personal victory.

THE POLITICS OF THE BID

European nations have dominated the elite club of privileged host nations, having been awarded the rights to play host to the world of soccer nine out of 16 tournaments. It has been the privilege of South America to host the lovers of soccer four times, including the first championship in 1930. The opportunity has gone thrice to North America -- once to the United States and twice to Mexico, the only country that has hosted the championships two times within two decades - 1970 and 1986. Africa and Oceania remain the two continents that have not tasted the glory and joy of having the world of soccer as their guests. Most nations no longer leave the struggle to win the bid to sports administrators. Governments and heads of state are involved in jockeying for the bid. Every sport, and especially soccer, has become so important and so is the opportunity to bring the world to your backyard to play, considering the huge opportunities global championships provide for business, tourism, cultural contacts and understanding.

CHAPTER TWELVE

2006 WORLD CUP BID

KEENER THAN EVER

The campaign for the bid to host the XVIII World Cup Championships began more than eight years before the tournament kicks off in the summer of the year 2006. Long-term plans and preparations are clearly reflective of how important the tournament has become. Nations aspiring for the bid are leaving no stones unturned in their efforts to land the golden opportunity.

British Prime Minister Tony Blair (left) accepts a soccer ball from outgoing FIFA President João Havelange at No. 10 Downing Street, London. Mr. Blair invited the FIFA chief to enhance England's chances of hosting the 2006 World Cup.
photo: "PA News" / Michael Stephens

CONTENDERS:

By the time the leaves and flowers that withered and faded in the autumn of 1997 had begun to turn green and bloom again in the spring of 1998, England and Germany had already confirmed their candidacies for the bid, but no less than a septuple of bids were still expected from at least three continents. Those who have signified their interest to land the rights to host the second World Cup tournament in the 21st century include Argentina, Brazil and Peru from South America. Egypt, Morocco and Nelson Mandela's South Africa are also in strong reckoning to jockey for the bid from the African continent. Australia is vying for the bid for Oceania. None of these nations is a pushover.

ENGLAND

Exponent of the modern game and proud maker of its first laws in 1863, England remains one of the most formidable contestants for the bid to host the World Cup in the year 2006. England has continued to blaze the trail. The growth of soccer in England is phenomenal and the popularity of the game is ever increasing. It is a household name everywhere in this great land, where soccer is not just a sport, but an industry and a big business with the leading clubs publicly quoted and traded in the stock market.

From 13 clubs, which in 1863 formed the Soccer Association in London, to 39 in 1870, England now boasts of 42,000 soccer clubs. Attendance at league games has also soared and by the end of 1995/96 season, a record 21.8 million spectators had watched the flambouyant and sometimes explosive league games. The terraces chalked up even higher attendance figures in the last two seasons.

England does not lack the sports facilities, efficient transport and security system, hotels and inns and more importantly, the public will to play host to the rest of the world. The English people have done it so well in the past. England parades some of the best and most famous soccer arenas in the world, although some of the sports grounds have seen violence and hooliganism in the past. However, if the way the English fans and their sports administrators acquitted themselves so creditably in their staging of the 1996 European Soccer Championship is a yardstick to go by, then the soccer world can rest assured it is coming into the warm, safe and competent hands of the English, come the year 2006.

Wembley, venue of 1966 World Cup Finals in London, England, verily has a stadium of legends. There are many more, including Anfield and Villa Park, which are not quite as famous. In an effort to provide more soccer grounds and give existing ones a facelift as part of their preparations for the 2006 World Cup, the English have spent about 600 million pounds. Wembley Stadium is also expected to be rebuilt.

Hosts of the eighth edition of the World Cup tournament in 1966, which they won, the English entered the race with experience, confidence and great hopes. They have very good reasons to expect the best out of the venture.

GOVERNMENT SUPPORT

England's bid to host the World Cup tournament has the blessings of both the people and government. In a solidarity message to England's campaign team for the 2006 bid, the British Prime Minister Tony Blair said, "the government supports England's World Cup bid wholeheartedly. We want to welcome you (the world) in 2006."

"Our commitment to sports is unrivaled, the Prime Minister stressed", adding "since 1996 we have invested, as a nation, over 1.8 billion pounds sterling in facilities, with a host of bold initiatives still to come." Confidently, Mr Blair said, "I believe that our country has the vision, the enthusiasm and the commitment to host an excellent World Cup in 2006."

The Prime Minister also emphasized the capacity of the English for "organisation and friendship", in a message that clearly demonstrated his strong support for England's bid. Mr. Blair's involvement was certainly not a mere lip service and did not end with rhetoric. He went several steps further to introduce some astute politicking into the bid. The Prime Minister invited outgoing FIFA President, Dr. Joao Havelange, to No.10 Downing Street, London on March 11, 1998 to press home the case of England. Mr. Blair assured the FIFA boss that "government is completely behind this bid."

The Prime Minister hosted Dr. Havelange in the presence of British Sports Minister Tony Banks and some officials of Lancaster Gate, the home of the English Football Association. Emerging from the 45-minute meeting, Havelange told journalists in French that "it is my personal wish" for England to host the

2006 World Cup. Although some people took Dr. Havelange's assertion with a grain of salt, the British government and people were encouraged by the FIFA chief's endorsement of their bid. Graham Kelly, the chief of the English Football Association, greeted Havelange's endorsement saying "this support is very welcome indeed". Also speaking in a similar vein, Alec McGivan, campaign director for England's 2006 World Cup bid said "it is a tremendous boost for us." England has continued to beef up its efforts to clinch the bid with the appointment of campaign ambassadors, including Bobby Charlton, Geoff Hurst, and Gary Lineker, all former World Cup stars who won laurels for their land. The adroit trio has brought global popularity and fortified the chances of England.

GERMAN PRESIDENTIAL BLESSINGS

German Chancellor Helmut Kohl

The German campaign has been less vocal, but by no means, less effective. The World Cup tournament has become so important that national leaders are now involved personally in the struggle to win the bid. Efforts of Deutscher Fussball-Bund (DFB), the German Football Association to win the 2006 bid have the blessings of the President of the Federal Republic of Germany, Roman Herzog. In a show of support for the DFB, Herzog assured the world that Germany's bid enjoys "the unqualified support of the whole country and my personal backing as well".

The German Chancellor Helmut Kohl, with a soccer ball in his right hand, added his voice of support for the bid saying "I wholeheartedly support the German Football Association in its effort to secure the organization of the 2006 World Cup". Turning to the world of soccer, Mr. Kohl said, "we will be good hosts and football fans from all over the world will meet fair and enthusiastic crowds". Mr. Kohl further assured the world that his government would "do everything possible to ensure that all participants, players and spectators will feel at home in Germany." The German soccer legend, Franz Beckenbauer, who was the skipper and coach of the triumphant West German World Cup squads of 1974 and 1990 respectively, and the President of the DFB, Egidius Braun, have also raised the German campaign to heights that are literally unbeatable.

Germany's bid appears to have the sympathy of the President of the Union of European Football Associations (UEFA) and FIFA Vice President Lennart Johansson, the sagacious Swede and his powerful clique in the corridors of power in FIFA's Soccer House in Zurich, Switzerland.

TITANS

The other caucus led by the outgoing FIFA boss, João Havelange, appears to include the newly elected President of FIFA, Joseph S. Blatter, the multilingual Swiss man, who has served the world of soccer since 1975, first as director of development projects and later as Secretary-General, with such dedication and conscientiousness that he has earned the accolade "Mr Football."

Havelange's clique and that of Johansson are rival groups. After the manner of astute politicians that both Havelange and Johansson are, they have not allowed their bickerings to spoil the broth at FIFA House, according to inside sources. It is an open secret that two of soccer's most powerful men have their personal differences, just as there is a gulf of style, views and modus operandi between their two caucuses. Make no mistake about it, the world of soccer is an arena of politics. It is a world of business. Nay, soccer is not just a sport, it is an industry. Alas, it is a terrain for dribbling, jockeying and outwitting your opponents, whether it is on the field of play or in the quest for the World Cup bid.

SOUTH AFRICA

The South Africans are no pushovers in the race for the 2006 bid. They are working very hard to spring a surprise. Like their failed bid to host the 2004 Olympic Games, the bid of the South

Africans is stoutly supported by President Nelson Mandela. Although his spirited challenge failed to wrest South Africa the bid for the XXVIII Olympiad, Dr. Mandela earned for his nation and himself the sympathy and support of observers all around the world at the end of the dramatic finish to the bid that returned the Olympic Games to Athens, Greece, home of the ancient games. Assuredly, South Africa can count on this goodwill as the nation enters the race for another global bid.

STATE AND SPORT

Sports are supposed to be administered by trained professionals without the interference of the meddling hands of the State. Though not expected to be as separate as the State should be from religion, sports administrators require some measure of autonomy to function properly. Sports have generated so much interest in all nations that some governments no longer leave their administration exclusively in the hands of professionals who are trained to perform the functions.

The bid to host the World Cup in the year 2006 has been competitive and political, and keener than ever. It has thrown open the question of whether governments should give sports professionals free hands to run the affairs of sports organisations and competitions and how much autonomy should be allowed.

BID SCHEDULE

The race for the bid is a long and arduous road to tread. FIFA has already provided a tentative timetable showing that it would issue the bid requirement by January 1999. It has also set a September 1999 deadline for the contending nations to submit their bid documents. FIFA inspection committee members are expected to visit the bidding countries by the end of May 2000 to assess the various facilities, including the venues in the prospective host cities where the World Cup games would be played, if a given nation wins the right to host the tournament.

The final decision on the eventual winners of the bid will be announced in June 2000. FIFA's Executive Committee, comprising 24 members, takes the final decision. The committee is made up of representatives from six continental Soccer Confederations, namely the African Football Confederation (CAF), the Asian Football Confederation (AFC), the Union of European Football Associations (UEFA), the Confederation of

North & Central American and Caribbean Football Associations (CONCACAF), the Oceania Football Association (OFC) and the Confederation of South American Football Associations (CONMEBOL).

Members of the FIFA Executive Committee

President:

       Joseph S. Blatter (Switzerland)

Immediate Past President:

       Dr. João Havelange (Brazil)

Vice Presidents:

       Julio Grondona (Argentina)
       David Will (Scotland)
       Lennart Johansson (Sweden)
       Issa Hayatou (Cameroon)
       Dr. Antonio Matarrese (Italy)
       Dr. Chung Mong-joon (Republic of Korea)
       Jack A Warner (Trinidad & Tobago)

Members:

       Dr. Viacheslav Koloskov (Russia)
       Abdullah K. Al-Dabal (Saudi Arabia)
       Slim Aloulou (Tunisia)
       Dr. Michel D'Hooghe (Belgium)
       Issac D. Sasso (Costa Rica)
       Ismail Bhamjee (Botswana)
       Gerard Mayer-Vorfelder (Germany)
       Dr. Nicolas Leoz (Paraguay)
       Richardo Terra Teixeira (Brazil)
       Per Ravn Omdal (Norway)
       Mohamed Bin Hammam (Qatar)
       Senes Erik (Turkey)
       Aimed Dacoit (Mali)
       Charles J. Dempsey BE (New Zealand)
       Chuck Blazer (USA)
       Worawi Makudi (Thailand)

Secretary General:

       To Be Announced

Immediate Past Secretary General: from 1981 to 1998

       Joseph S. Blatter (Switzerland)

DECISION

The race for winning the rights to host the World Cup soccer championships has always been a great competition itself, engendering sportsmanly rivalry as well as political moves and government interventions in some nations. Both strongmen of the FIFA House, Dr. Havelange and his successor, Mr. Blatter, have at various times spoken about the 2006 bid in a manner that showed they have a soft spot for South Africa. Havelange also endorsed the bid of England. In March 1998 Havelange said in London "It is my personal wish" for England to host the 2006 World Cup.

The choice of the World Cup bid winner depends, to a large extent, on the new leadership of FIFA. Mr. Joseph Blatter was elected president following the withdrawal of Johansson during the second ballot after Mr. Blatter won the first vote 111-80.

At press time Argentina, Australia, Brazil, Ecuador, Egypt, Morocco and Peru had not announced their candidacies and not much was known about their plans for the bid.

Glossary

Ace - A star player.

Advantage rule - A decision of the referee not to stop play for an infringement if the offending team is likely to benefit.

AFC - the Asian Football Confederation.

Amateur - A player who does not get paid for participating in a sport.

Assist - To put a teammate in an advantageous position or to be instrumental to the scoring of a goal.

Association Football - The official name for organized soccer at the national state, provincial or city level.

Attempt - An effort to score a goal.

Attendance - The number of spectators who watch a game from the terraces or bleachers.

Award - The decision of a referee for or against a player or team. For example: a penalty award.

Away Goals Rule - A rule used to break a tie, especially in round-robin tournaments or league games when two teams are level on points.

Back Pass - A pass in the direction of one's own end of the field.

Balloon the ball - To play the ball into the air far and away from the pitch and out of play for ball kids to find.

Book a player - violation of a law of the game recorded against a player. This is done by the referee who takes the name of the offending player and his jersey number.

Boot - To kick the ball far away.

Box - The penalty area.

CAF - African Football Confederation.

Cap - A player wins a cap or is capped when he plays an international game.

Caution - An official warning by the referee.

Centre circle - The central part of the field or circle where the kickoff takes place before a game or after a goal is scored.

Centre halfback - The middle position among halfbacks.

Challenge - To contest the ball with another player or to lock horns with another team.

Cheer crew - A corps of usually girls, but sometimes boys, whose duty is to lustily cheer and spur their teams into action and goal scoring.

Chip - A careful kick usually vaulted over the head of an onrushing player.

Clearance - An action of a player to put the ball away from his danger zone.

CONCACAF - the Confederation of North & Central American and Caribbean Football Associations.

CONMEBOL - the Confederation of South American Football Associations.

Cross - A pass to the centre of the field or goal-mouth from either the left or right flank.

Cross Bar - The horizontal pole that connects the goal posts.

Dark Horse - A team that is lowly rated at the beginning of a competition, but performs far better than expected.

Direct Free Kick - A free kick from which a goal may be scored.

Dissent - Showing disagreement with a referee's decision.

Double - To win two championships or titles in a season.

Dribble - The act of moving the ball artfully past an opponent.

Eighteen - Penalty area.

Equalize - To score a goal that makes the scores even.

Esprit de Corps - Team spirit, teamwork.

Finishing - refers to how well or poorly a team completes an effort to score.

Flag Kick - A corner kick.

Flank - The extreme right and left corners or sides of a soccer field.

Fourth Official - the number 4 man in the officiating team.

Full Back - One of two defenders playing from either side of the goal area.

Goal Aggregate - The total number of goals scored by one team compared with scores of other teams in a competition.

Goal Difference - The number of goals scored by a team minus those it conceded.

Goal Net - A net of nylon attached to the goal posts, crossbar and ground behind the goal to ascertain that a goal is actually scored.

Goal Tender - The first player in the order of position, who watches and prevents the ball from getting into his net, goalkeeper.

Half Backs - The three positions that link the rearguard and attack.

Half Time - The interval or period of time between the two halves of a game.

Hang on to a lead - To defend a goal or prevent the opponent from scoring.

Hat trick - The scoring of three goals by a player in one match.

Home and Away - A two-game series with one match played on a given team's home ground and the second on the opponent's arena.

IFAB - The global body that makes the laws of soccer.

Indirect Free Kick - A free kick from which a goal may not be scored directly by the player who takes the kick.

Infringement - A foul or violation of the laws of the game.

Injury time - is the time allowed by the referee at the end of either half to make up for time lost because of an injury or any other stoppage of the game.

In to touch - Out of play.

Joust - Also known as a tournament.

Kick off - The pass, signalling the beginning of a game.

Laws of the game - The code regulating the conduct of a game of soccer, its players, and officials.

League - is a competition in which all teams involved play against one another with the team that chalks up the highest number of points emerging as the winner.

Linksman - A player, who provides the much-needed connection between the rearguard and the attack.

Lob - To hit the ball in such a way that it descends gradually into the opponent's goal area.

Lose control - to give up possession of the ball to an opponent.

Mark - To confront or prevent an opponent's incursion into a player's own side of the field.

Midfielder - a schemer or player who operates in the middle of field, distributing the ball and providing support for the attack and rearguard.

Net the ball - to score a goal.

OFC - the Oceania Football Association.

Offside - means the decision of the referee to penalize a player for lurking behind the opposing players, defending a given goal post, to gain undue advantage.

Offside trap - A defensive tactic, in which players of a team surge forward intently to stem the incessant forays of an attacking machine. This intent is to create a foul or situation for attackers to be caught behind the defenders.

Out of play - means the ball has gone outside the field or area in which it may be played.

Overlap - the initiative taken by fullbacks in moving into the attack to support efforts to score goals.

Own goal - a defensive error, resulting in a player deflecting the ball into his own net.

Pace - the rate or speed at which a game is played. It is either fast or slow.

Pass - the kicking of the ball from one player to another of the same team.

Penalty arc - Is the area surrounding the edge of the penalty spot.

Post - The goal post.

Promotion - An act of elevation which takes a team from a lower division to a higher one, usually in a league.

Pushover - A team that can be easily defeated.

Qualifier - A preliminary game to decide which team plays in the final stages of a competition.

Qualifying Rounds - Games played to eliminate and determine which countries go into the final stages of a tournament.

Rearguard - The part of a soccer team that prevents opponents from scoring.

Referee - The number one man in the officiating team whose duty is to ensure that players keep the rules and regulations of the game or are penalized for violation.

Relegation - An act of demotion requiring a team to be brought down from a higher division to a lower one at the end of a soccer season.

Round robin - is an arrangement for a competition, in which each team plays against all the others until the emergence of a winner.

Rout - to defeat.

Run of play - is the proceedings of a game or how it went.

Save - stoppage of a goal-bound shot from going into one's net.

Sell a dummy - A ploy, usually a gesticulation or body movement made by a player in a dribbling run, to fake going in a direction opposite from the one he intends in a bid to outwit an opponent.

Sideline - touch line.

Six-yard box - the inner third part of the eighteen closest to the goal posts or goal area.

Skipper - Captain of a team.

Spot kick - penalty kick.

Star-studded team - A team full of very famous players.

Stopper - A defender with a knack for preventing attackers from invading his goal area.

Striker - A player in the heart of the attack, who usually takes the most shots at goal.

Substitute - A player who replaces another in the course of the game, usually the decision of the coach or team manager; substitution.

Swoop - A sudden attack.

Tackle - An effort made by a player to snatch the ball from an opponent.

Take by storm - Take (defenders) by surprise.

Teamwork - The cooperation of players of a team with one another towards ensuring victory.

Tempo - the rate or speed at which a game is played. It is either fast or slow.

Throw-in - The use of the hands or feet to return the ball to play when it has crossed a touch line.

Tournament - A competition or sports festival.

Transfer - The decision of a team to trade or allow a player to go from one club to another.

Ubiquitous player - Is one who roves round, going everywhere on the field.

UEFA - the Union of European Football Associations.

Unanimous decision - A decision reached by all members of the officiating team, without the dissent of one.

Underdog - A team that enters a competition with little chance of winning.

Unlawful conduct - Behavior at variance with the laws of the game.

Volley - A shot taken, while the ball is still in the air.

Wallop - To defeat decisively.

Whirlwind attack - A massive onslaught (of attackers).

Wild card - Unpredictable. A wild card final.

Wingers - Attackers who play at the right and left flanks of a field and usually create goal-mouth melee with their lobs from the flanks.

Wizardry - Great skills in the playing of a sport; artistry.

World Cup - The global soccer competition which determines the country that has the best soccer team in the world. It is a quadrennial tournament.

[E]xchanges - The number of minutes controlled by each side in a game. For example, even exchanges, as in an exchange of fire in war.

[E]xtra time - The 2 x 15 minutes allowed beyond the 90-minute regulation time to decide the winner, following a draw or equal score.

Yeoman - A hard working player, such as a yeoman in the heart of a rearguard.

Yellow Card - A caution indicated with a yellow card shown by the referee to a player for a minor violation of a law of the game.

Zonal play - A system of play in which each player is assigned responsibility for a given part of the field to operate from or guard.

[Danger] zone - Penalty area.

1998 WORLD CUP CHAMPIONSHIP
(*Continued from Page 41*)

Brazil 3   Morocco 0

Austria 1   Chile 1

Italy 3   Cameroon 0

Denmark 1   South Africa 1

France 4   Saudi Arabia 0

Nigeria 1   Bulgaria 0

Paraguay 0   Spain 0

Belgium 2   Mexico 2

Netherlands 5   South Korea 0

Yugoslavia 2   Germany 2

Iran 2   USA 1

Croatia 1   Japan 0

Argentina 5   Jamaica 0

Columbia 1   Tunisia 0

Romania 2   England 1

Italy 2   Austria 1

Chile 1   Cameroon 1

GREATEST UPSETS:

Norway 2   Brazil 1

Morocco 3   Scotland 0

First teams to qualify for the second round:
BRAZIL, FRANCE and NIGERIA.

STAR PLAYERS OF THE FIRST ROUND:

Romario, Bebeto, Roberto Carlos (BRAZIL), Gabriel Batistuta (ARGENTINA), Hagi and Adrian Ilie (ROMANIA), Mijatovic (YUGOSLAVIA), Luis Hernandez (MEXICO), Chris Dugarry, Pierre Issa, Thierry Henry (FRANCE), Marcelo Salas (CHILE), Celestine Babayaro, Taribo West and Sunday Oliseh (NIGERIA), Alan Shearer, Michael Owen and Sol Campbell (ENGLAND), Jim Leighton (SCOTLAND) and Di Biagio, Christian Vieri and Roberto Baggio (ITALY).

ABOUT THE AUTHOR

Fidelis W. Iyebote is an accomplished and versatile journalist of international repute. His professional career is adorned with skills and experience acquired in North America, Europe, Asia, and Africa. He has exercised his craft in three continents and his articles on environmental, political, religious, sports, and economic issues have been published in the United States, Canada, Denmark, Germany, and Switzerland among others.

A distinguished scholar, Iyebote was designated an Editorial Writer's Fellow of the *Knight Center for Specialized Journalism at the University of Maryland College of Journalism*, College Park, Maryland, U.S.A. on December 5, 1997. He was a 1989 winner of the *Netherlands Christian Foundation* Fellowship Award held at the *Asian Institute for Christian Communications*, Chiang Mai, Thailand.

Another feather was added to Fidelis' glowingly ornamented hat in the autumn of 1986 when he earned the *American Society of Newspaper Editors'* (ASNE) Fellowship Award held at the *Fletcher School of Law and Diplomacy, Tufts University,* Medford, Massachusetts, U.S.A. in cooperation with *Harvard University.*

Iyebote, had earlier, in 1985 been granted the News Service Journalism Fellowship Award organized jointly by the *Danish International Development Agency* (DANIDA) and *Denmark's National Committee of the United Nations Educational, Scientific and Cultural Organization* (UNESCO), held at *Ritzau Bureau,* the Danish National News Service.

A mass communicator, Fidelis' professional experience includes stints on various newspapers, radio, television and magazines including *U.S. News & World Report*, publishers of the *U.S. News* magazine, *America's Best Colleges' Guide, America's Graduate School Directory*, and *Great Vacation Drives,* a travel guide.

Fidelis served as Washington Correspondent of Canada's *Ottawa Times*. He has also worked in the capacity of bureau chief for two national dailies and as editor of *Banner News Service.*

The articles of Iyebote have been published and read in *Kontakt* magazine at Copenhagen, Denmark, *Ecumenical News Service,* Geneva, Switzerland, *IDEA News Service* in Wetzlar, Germany, and *Agence Telegraphique Suisse,* the Swiss Agency in Berne, Switzerland. Iyebote is an author of educational books. He is also a prolific sports writer and a master of the art.